CHICKEN
& Other Fowl

CHICKEN

& OTHER FOWL

JOHN TORODE

photographs
by Jason Lowe

FIREFLY BOOKS

The humble chicken (I believe humble is the right word for chicken, underrated another) is by far the most-consumed meat in the modern world. It is fast to grow, easy to keep, multifunctional (chickens lay eggs too, after all) and, vegetarians aside, appeals to nearly every cuisine in the world as well as most religions.

I have always believed that if you can roast a chicken you will survive. It's a simple skill that gives you freedom. Use a different stuffing, vary the side dishes and sauces, or take that bird, rub it with spices and cook it in a tagine — yes, it is still roasting, just in a different way. And if you swap the chick for a guinea fowl, pheasant or duck, the meal will be a little different again. Master the roast chicken and you will quickly come to understand your oven and your taste buds, and from there the world is your oyster.

I was very young when I made gravy next to my grandma in Maitland, just outside Newcastle in Australia. She cooked simply but with real confidence, the confidence that comes with knowledge and practice. Her repertoire (if you can call it that) was not huge and that is why she has always been an inspiration. She knew how to roast the perfect chicken; she knew how to make soup (fabulous asparagus and chicken soup); she cooked celebration meals (roast duck and various other birds) as well as great family stews and pies. Oh, those pies — I am still trying to get mine to taste as good. She also knew what to do with the bits that were left over: big sandwiches made with the cold meat, stuffing and gelatinous gravy, plus fritters, salads, soups and pasta dishes. She was good, and I hope that with this book I am able to impart some of her confidence in the kitchen so that you too can cook with ease.

Home cooking is very different from restaurant cooking. Restaurants use formulaic recipes and employ chefs who have been honing the same dish for years. Although some of the recipes in this book have featured on the menus of my restaurants, this is not a restaurant cookbook. It's a people cookbook. It starts with the basics, jumps around a little and moves onto more complex recipes and techniques. The aim is to give you the confidence to cook a bird with style, whether it be a humble yet delicious roast chicken or salt-and-pepper quail with sweet chili sauce. My advice is to get joy from the basics first — learn them, do them well. Some recipes you will love and some you will not — we are all different and we all like different things. Except a roast chicken, that is. We all love, love, love the roast chicken!

BIRDS OF A FEATHER

Many fowl these days are farm raised, and history suggests that domesticating birds for eating has been going on for thousands of years. They are no problem to transport so are easy to take to market, and should you have one male and a few hens it is not that difficult to breed your own flock and feed the family.

Before the advent of large farms producing young fowl specifically for the table, a chicken's life was destined to be spent laying eggs. Whether or not to kill and cook one of the family's chickens would have been a difficult choice and the act was often restricted to celebratory meals. Usually the birds chosen had spent many years laying eggs, hence the expression "a tough old bird." Older cookbooks therefore tend to concentrate on boiling, braising, stewing and pot-roasting chicken — all long cooking processes that break down the tough meat fibers and encourage absorption of flavors from the other ingredients. It is only in the modern world that recipes call for tender chicken breasts, and birds stripped of their skin to appease dietary concerns.

The edible birds are many, so let's start by separating the domesticated from the wild. Birds that are farm raised, growing and maturing well in a controlled environment to produce meat and eggs, are termed poultry. They don't need to be matured after slaughter, are easy to process and transport and have a good shelf life. Chicken, turkey, duck and goose are familiar examples. However, any fowl that you buy — be it guinea fowl, quail, partridge or pheasant — is poultry. This is because only "inspected" farm-raised birds can be legally offered for sale. For a true wild game bird you have to shoot it yourself.

The domestic chicken is now a superpower, its breeds mostly a number or code on the side of a carton, not a name. Chicken breeders continue to try to perfect their breeds using all sorts of methods so the birds can grow quickly and produce huge yields at minimal cost. The success of the chicken and our appetite for it is, after all, down to cost and accessibility.

In a supermarket today you will usually find whole chickens weighing 4½–7 lb (2–3 kg). These will be "roasters" (3–5 months old). The younger and smaller "broiler-fryers" (about 7 weeks old and 2½–4½ lb/1.1–2 kg in weight) may also be offered for sale. The smallest birds are poussins, also called squab chickens (about 4 weeks old and 1 lb/450 g in weight), and Rock Cornish game hens (5–6 weeks old and 1½–2 lb/680–900 g in weight). The meat of these miniature chickens is more delicate than that of older birds.

At about 5 months of age, female chickens start laying eggs and males become sexually mature. These male "roosters" have tough, stringy meat and aren't that good to eat, so when bred for the table a male chicken is normally castrated at 15–18 weeks, then allowed to grow big and plump. The resulting bird is called a capon and has lots of tender, succulent meat. It is good for stuffing and roasting. Stewing chickens, at 4–8 lb (1.8–3.6 kg) in weight, are usually older egg-laying hens. As their name suggests, they are best slow-cooked by a moist heat method and have plenty of flavor.

For all breeds of poultry, the female is considered to be the better domestic bird because she has a good temperament (quieter and better behaved than the male) and grows more evenly and not too fast, which would make the meat tough.

These days chicken, turkey, duck and other fowl are farmed in huge quantities and are available year-round. The U.S. is the world's largest poultry producer and each American eats an average of 70 lb (31.5 kg) of chicken meat per year, plus 250 eggs. The farming of birds is a sensitive subject to some, but if you have been given the facts about the different methods of farm-raising poultry then it is up to you to make your choices.

Free-range poultry is allowed access to the outdoors, which in practice means that the door to the coop must be open so the birds can roam and forage if they wish. Organic poultry is fed only certified organic feed, raised without cages in housing that allows outdoor access and not given antibiotics or other drugs to promote growth. Kosher poultry is specially raised, usually free range or free-roaming within the housing, fed a grain diet and ritually slaughtered under rabbinical supervision. Halal chickens are hand-slaughtered by someone of the Islamic faith. Poultry labeled "natural," as currently defined by the USDA, should contain no artificial ingredients or added color and should be only minimally processed; however, there is ongoing debate about the use of this term and its accuracy.

Generally speaking, free-range, organic and kosher poultry is of high quality and has a better flavor than cage- or pen-raised fowl. Kosher poultry may taste a bit salty, because salting is required in the kosher process.

Unlike chicken and other familiar domesticated fowl, farm-raised game birds are usually not crowded into pens but are raised under free-range conditions that mimic the wild. Farmed game birds are milder in flavor and less lean than their wild counterparts, which need to be matured, or hung, for a time after slaughter to tenderize their meat and enhance the flavor. Wildfowl also need some fat to be added when cooking, by basting or barding. Older game birds, whether farm raised or wild, are best braised or stewed.

BIRDS OF A FEATHER

 CHICKEN
Today's commercial chickens are an amalgamation of various breeds, bred to grow quickly and produce the right amounts of soft meat that we all love so much. Very rarely do we buy chickens according to their breed, mainly because there was no traditional breed that produced huge breasts (stop the giggling) and long, fleshy legs. The French, however, prize some breeds and at the top of the table is the long-legged Poulet de Bresse, which has a very long, thin breast and a deep, almost gamy flavor. The California Poulet Bleu, or Blue Foot, is a Bresse-style chicken with a good firm texture and similar gamy taste.

 DUCK
There are many types of duck hunted in the wild, but those raised for food are all descended from either the mallard or the Muscovy. For example, the Long Island duck, one of the most common domesticated ducks, with rich dark meat, is a descendant of the Chinese Peking or Pekin duck, a type of mallard. The Muscovy duck, which is leaner than a mallard and with a good flavor, is very popular in Europe, particularly in France. It has been crossed with the Pekin to produce a new breed, the Moulard duck. Breasts from the Moulard, called magrets, are large and succulent. The Moulard is also used to produce foie gras in California and in the eastern U.S. and Canada.

 GOOSE
The temperamental goose is a majestic bird. Of the wildfowl hunted in North America, the large Canada goose is the most common. While wild goose is extremely lean, its larger domesticated counterpart is extremely fatty. The heavier the goose, the bigger the frame it will need to get off the ground; it will also carry more fat. However, its copious fat is just under the skin and is easily rendered during roasting, leaving you with the bonus of a delicious cooking fat for potatoes and confit. The meat on a goose is entirely dark and when roasted is more similar to roast beef than roast chicken or turkey. There is not a great deal of meat on the bird, but it is richly flavored. Younger geese are more tender than older birds.

GROUSE
Grouse is a true game bird, only found wild. Many people consider it to be the finest of all game birds — in Britain, the opening of the grouse-shooting season in August is known as "The Glorious Twelfth." Grouse love cold weather, almost subarctic, and exist primarily in the northern hemisphere. Those in North America include the ruffed grouse and the sage grouse. Ptarmigan is another member of the grouse family. The meat of a grouse is dark and has a fine distinctive flavor; like all true game birds it is very lean so needs to be barded before cooking.

GUINEA FOWL

The domesticated guinea fowl, or guinea hen, is a shadow of its wild former self. Once a big, long-necked bird with a skinny body and quite a nutty flavor, the guinea fowl as we know it now is slightly smaller than a chicken, with a thin skin and tender, delicate meat. Compared to chicken, the meat is drier, slightly darker and redder, and a bit more gamy in flavor — more similar to pheasant although milder.

PARTRIDGE

In North America, several wild game birds, such as the ruffed grouse and bobwhite quail, are erroneously called partridge, whereas only the European gray, or gray-legged, and red-legged are true partridges. The former was imported from Hungary and is hunted here. Its domesticated cousin, the chukar partridge, is somewhat larger although it is still a small bird. The meat is tender and mild, much less flavorful than its wild counterpart.

PHEASANT

This medium-sized game bird is widely farm raised in North America and in Europe, but like many other domesticated game birds its mild, delicate flavor is nowhere near as good as the deliciously rich, gamy meat of the wild variety. In Europe, the wild birds are normally hung to age them, which makes them more tender and enhances their flavor. Hen pheasants have large breasts and skinny legs – supermodels, if you will.

PIGEON AND SQUAB

There are thousands of breeds of pigeon, but few are suitable for eating. Wild wood pigeons are hunted in Europe and you sometimes find these in gourmet markets, imported from Scotland. Doves are another wild member of the pigeon family. The domesticated pigeon is the squab, which is widely available. It is a young bird that has never flown, so its dark, juicy meat is very tender. Squab breasts are best cooked no more than medium-rare to retain their succulence. Because squabs are small you should allow one per person.

QUAIL

The quail is a land-dwelling, nonmigratory bird that is valued both for its sweet and tender meat and for its tiny, delicate eggs with their pretty speckled shells. In many parts of North America quail is a popular game bird (sometimes wrongly called partridge). The small birds are widely farm raised so are easily obtainable. Unlike other game birds, the domesticated version is just as good — as long as quail has plenty of land to run around in it produces deep-flavored meat, fleshy legs and small, delicious breasts.

TURKEY

The turkey is a large, nonflying bird native to North America which as legend has it was eaten at the first Thanksgiving dinner by the Pilgrims and their Native American guests. Wild turkeys — even those that are farm raised — have much darker, leaner, more savory meat than fully domesticated turkeys, with their plump breasts of tender white meat. Most supermarket turkeys are the Broad-Breasted White variety, but heritage or heirloom breeds such as Bourbon Red, Jersey Buff, Narragansett and Black Spanish are gaining in popularity. Their meat is firmer, darker and more flavorful than that of standard turkeys, with smaller breasts and larger thighs.

SHOPPING

When it comes to shopping for poultry the general rule is common sense. Check the expiry date — unless you are going to cook the bird right away, this date shouldn't be too near — and be sure the packaging is intact and that there is nothing unusual or suspect about the bird's appearance.

Look for plump, healthy, clean birds with even color under the skin. The skin of whole birds should be intact — there should be no tears in it at all — and unblemished.

Also choose a bird that looks in proportion. I know that sounds a bit strange, but a chicken should not look scrawny, a duck should not look fatty, a pheasant should not be a big plump thing and a turkey should not be round like a bowling ball — it should have a turkey shape.

If possible buy fresh poultry, which in fact will probably have been frozen (despite being called "fresh," most birds are kept at below freezing point for several weeks after slaughter). If not labeled fresh, the bird will have been stored at a lower freezing temperature for an indefinite period and this will adversely affect the flavor. You can taste the difference between them.

For the best flavor you should look for premium poultry (free range, organic or kosher). This is more expensive, and not all of us can afford to spend a lot on ingredients, but look at it this way: maybe it's better to have chicken less often, and when you do to enjoy the very best.

CUTTING UP A BIRD

A bird has a few bits to it, but fortunately all birds have the same bits. Some of the best are inside the bird and most prized is the liver. When buying a bird you will often find a plastic bag inside containing the heart, gizzard and neck; these are great for making stock.

The hen of any bird has the plumpest breasts — nothing unusual there! The breasts are guarded by the wings and above that you will find the opening to the neck. Remember: the wing end is the neck end; the other end is the cavity. Stuffing can go in the neck end or cavity, or you can just put flavorings in the cavity.

It is much more economical to buy a whole bird, cut it up yourself and get the most out of it, rather than buying parts in a pack. Learning to cut up a chicken is one of the most useful skills a cook can have and is easy with a bit of practice.

To do it, place the bird breast up on a board. Pull one wing out and slice through the joint halfway down the wing to remove the pointed part. Repeat on the other side.

Turn the bird so the cavity is nearest to you, then take the end of a leg in each hand — this needs to be a firm hold, not a flimsy attempt! Pull the legs away from the bird so that they stretch out; do not snap the joint or tear the skin. Then use the knife to cut through the skin between the breast and each of the legs.

Pinch the skin at the cavity end together, holding it closed. Make a cut above the pinch but underneath the point of the breastbone, and follow the breast line along on one side to meet the cut you made above the leg. Repeat on the other side.

Hold the breast firmly from above with one hand. Pick the chicken up and rest it back on the wings. With your other hand, pull the legs down firmly, snapping the backbone. Cut through the area where the bone snapped. You now have a crown (the whole breast on the bone) plus the legs and thighs attached to the backbone.

Take a leg in each hand, skin side toward the board, and snap the legs toward each other — this dislocates the legs from the backbone. Cut each leg off at the thigh along the natural split.

Sit the crown so the wing joints are near you and lift the skin to reveal the wishbone. Cut in between the meat and the wishbone in a neat V-shape so that you can pull the wishbone out. Stretch the skin tightly across the top and mold the breast back into shape. On one side, following the line of the bone, run the knife through to the bone and let the weight of the breast half help it fall off the bone while you encourage its release with your knife. This is easiest using a quick flicking motion directed away from you.

When the breast has come away, hold it with the wing down and cut through the wing joint. Repeat on the other side and you are done.

HOW TO USE THE RECIPES

The recipes in this book are simple and should be easy for you to follow. I wanted them to be short and inspiring, rather than dictatorial.

The number of birds at the top of each recipe is an indication of portions — but just an indication. The number of servings depends so much on appetite.

 means a dish should serve four people, while means a dish will serve two to four people, depending on the size of the portions and how hungry you all are.

A few other points: When a recipe calls for salt and pepper I assume you will use freshly ground black pepper. However, I often use other types of pepper and when these are required they will be specified in the ingredients list. When it's best to use flaky sea salt rather than finer salt, the recipe will say so.

Where a recipe calls for vegetable oil you can use any light, neutral-tasting oil; in these cases the flavor of olive oil will be too distinctive. If it's important to use extra-virgin olive oil the ingredients list will specify this.

Eggs in all recipes are large, unless otherwise specified.

Some of the sauce and dressing recipes will produce more than you need for one day, because it's often easier to make a good batch and have some leftovers on standby for subsequent meals.

Please do remember that there are plenty of variables when it comes to food and cooking, from your oven to the size of your "handful" to how sharp your knife is.

My advice is to practice. Pick a recipe and cook it — not once, not twice, but four or five times. Get confident with it, feel it, and change or adapt it to suit your own taste. Don't think that when you cook, everything should just work, and if not that the recipe is at fault. Concert pianists always make a mistake or two the first few times they play a new piece of music. It is only with practice, confidence and knowledge that you will become a great cook, regardless of the size of your repertoire. Remember my grandma, who was the finest cook I know.

The great soups of the world have never been made from scraps or leftovers, as many people think. Great soups are made with the finest ingredients and are packed full of goodness. The Italians used to boil meats, serve the broth to the kings and queens and then throw the meat to the peasants. For the great Jewish staple, chicken soup, a whole chicken is simmered so that all its flavor is extracted; the bird itself is dispensed with. Even for classic cream of chicken soup you should use only the very best. Don't skimp: buy quality, cook it carefully and you will have a good pot of soup that satisfies and heals.

Traditionally, all chickens were kept for laying eggs and at the end of the yearly laying cycle became "stewing" hens. These made the best stock. There are two basic types of chicken stock: brown chicken stock, where the bones are roasted before simmering, and white chicken stock, which is more common. The canned bouillon and bouillon cubes and powders that you buy from a supermarket will have a white chicken stock flavor. Many people use the bones from roast chicken for stock-making. Although the bird has been roasted the result will be more like white stock, because the bones themselves have not been colored.

soups and stocks

CLASSIC CHICKEN STOCK

MAKES ABOUT 4½ QUARTS
  OR 18 CUPS

1 whole chicken, split in half
  down the center and rinsed
  under cold water
2 carrots, peeled
1 leek, split lengthwise
some herb stalks
2 bay leaves
2 whole cloves
10 black peppercorns
a little salt

This recipe uses a whole chicken. You could use chicken bones instead, although they won't give the same rich flavor.

Put everything in a really big pot and add about 5 quarts (20 cups) of cold water. Bring slowly to a boil, then reduce the heat to a simmer and cook for 2 hours.

Remove the pot from the heat and let the stock cool overnight.

The next day, bring the stock slowly to a boil again. Remove from the heat and let cool slightly, then strain the liquid through a clean dish towel into a large bowl.

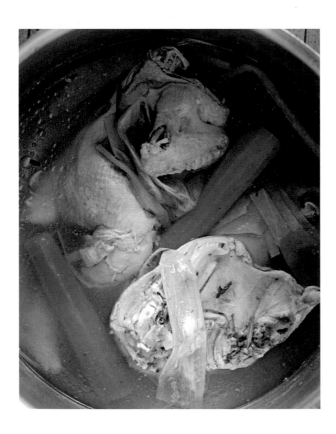

GAME STOCK

MAKES ABOUT 2 QUARTS
  OR 8 CUPS

2¼ lb (1 kg) bones from game
  fowl, such as pheasant,
  partridge, guinea fowl or
  whatever you have, including
  necks and wings
vegetable oil
1 onion
1 leek
½ fennel bulb
1 celery stalk
1 carrot
¼ head of cabbage
2 garlic cloves
handful of fresh herbs, such
  as parsley, chives, sage and
  basil, including the stems
1 star anise
10 black peppercorns, crushed
salt
handful of ice cubes

Preheat the oven to 425°F (220°C). Chop the bones so that they are roughly the same size as the palm of your hand. Put them in a heavy roasting pan and mix with a little vegetable oil. Roast until well colored all over, about 40 minutes, moving them around once during cooking.

While the bones are roasting, cut all the vegetables and garlic into 1-inch (2.5 cm) chunks, keeping the cabbage separate. In a large pot, gently sweat the onion, leek, fennel, celery, carrot and garlic in a little oil until soft, keeping the pot covered and making sure the vegetables do not color.

Drain off any excess oil from the bones, then add them to the vegetables in the pot. Pour in 4 quarts (16 cups) of cold water and add the cabbage, herbs, spices and a little salt. Throw in the ice cubes, which will set the fat into a "raft" on the surface of the liquid. Skim off this raft, then bring the liquid to a boil. Keep skimming off any fat that forms on the surface.

After 10 minutes of constant skimming, turn the heat down so the liquid is just barely moving and let cook for 3 hours.

Remove the pot from the heat and let cool. Then strain the stock, pressing all the liquid from the vegetables and bones. Discard these. The stock should be reasonably clear, brown in color and very flavorsome.

CREAM OF CHICKEN SOUP

SERVES

5 cups chicken stock (page 20)
7 tbsp butter
$^2/_3$ cup all-purpose flour
1 cup milk
$^1/_2$ cup cream
salt and white pepper

The classics are always the best, and cream of chicken soup is a beauty. It is so simple to make and keeps well. If you are a purist then the stock should be homemade, although canned bouillon will work too. For a fancy version, add a pinch of minced fresh tarragon or some strips of cooked chicken.

Bring the stock to a boil in a saucepan. Meanwhile, in a separate saucepan — a large, heavy-based one — melt the butter over low heat, then add a large pinch of white pepper and some salt. Let the butter start to bubble, then add the flour and reduce the heat. Now you need to keep stirring: the mix (or roux, as it is called in French) will slowly turn white.

Start slowly ladling the hot stock into the pan of roux, stirring the mixture as it starts to boil. I mean really stir. Keep on stirring as you add more stock so that there are no lumps. (If you do have lumps and cannot stir them out, use an immersion blender.)

When all the stock has been added, bring back to a boil. Add the milk and heat, then taste the soup and season. It should taste of chicken. If it doesn't, you can add some chicken bouillon powder or crumbled bouillon cube to heighten the flavor. Just before you are ready to serve, add the cream.

CHICKEN AND ASPARAGUS SOUP

SERVES

7 tbsp butter
30 large asparagus spears
2 potatoes, peeled and diced
2 leeks, diced
2 shallots, diced
6 cups chicken stock (page 20)
extra-virgin olive oil, for
  sprinkling
salt and pepper

The best soups are made with the finest ingredients. This one — seasoned properly, finished with some fabulous olive oil, then savored with really fresh bread — is fantastic.

Melt the butter in a large, heavy-based saucepan over low heat. Snap the tough ends from the asparagus stalks and add the tough parts to the butter. Season generously with salt and pepper and add the potatoes and leeks. Cook for 2 minutes, then add the shallots and cook for 4 minutes longer.

Stir in the stock and bring to a boil. Cook over medium heat until the potatoes are soft, about 15 minutes. Transfer the soup to a food processor and blend to a fine puree.

Strain the soup through a fine sieve into a clean saucepan, pressing all the flavorsome juices from the fibrous remains, which you should then discard.

Cut the top 2 inches (5 cm) off the asparagus spears. Cook these tips in a pan of boiling water for 4 minutes. Add the rest of the asparagus stalks to your soup pan and cook for the same amount of time.

Blend the soup again until smooth. To serve, ladle the soup into six bowls, garnish with the cooked asparagus tips and sprinkle with a little extra-virgin olive oil.

Tip: this soup is great with croutons. To make them, cut some stale bread into bite-size chunks and put them on a baking sheet — don't add any oil. Bake them in a preheated 325°F (160°C) oven until colored, about 15 minutes.

CHICKEN SOUP WITH MATZO BALLS

SERVES

1 large stewing chicken, cut
  into 12 pieces
3 carrots, peeled
2 onions
1 celery stalk
1 tsp black peppercorns
3 eggs
handful of chopped fresh
  parsley

MATZO BALLS
10 large matzo crackers
1 onion, finely diced
a little vegetable oil
2 eggs
a little matzo meal (or ground
  matzo crackers)
pinch of grated nutmeg
salt and pepper

This recipe is all about the goodness of the broth, the flavor of the soup and the great matzo balls. The "golden egg," which is an egg that is still inside a female chicken, is the prize of any Jewish family's soup pot. To replicate this, I float hard-boiled egg yolks in the soup.

Put the chicken in a bowl of cold water, add some salt and let soak for 20 minutes; drain and throw the water away (this will wash off any blood and prevents the soup from being cloudy).

Put the chicken in a soup pot with all the vegetables and the peppercorns. Add enough water to cover the chicken by 4 inches (10 cm). Bring to a boil, then reduce the heat and simmer for 5–6 hours, adding more water when needed to keep the chicken covered with liquid.

Meanwhile, in a large saucepan, hard-cook the eggs for 8–10 minutes. Drain and let cool in cold water. Peel off the shells and remove the whites, leaving the cooked yolks whole. Set aside.

Strain the broth and season as needed. Pour into a clean pan (reheat just before serving). Take out 1 cup of the broth for cooking the matzo balls and put it in another saucepan.

Leaving the matzo crackers in the sealed plastic they come in, crunch them up into little pieces. Open the pack and drop them into a bowl of water, then drain immediately.

Soften the onion in the oil without letting it color. Put the onion in a bowl and add the rest of the ingredients for the matzo balls, including the crushed crackers. Mix to a paste, adding more matzo meal if needed. Roll into marble-sized balls. Drop into the reserved broth, bring to a boil and cook for 15–20 minutes.

Add the matzo balls with their broth and the hard-boiled egg yolks to the rest of the hot broth in a large tureen. Scatter chopped parsley over the top and serve.

STRACCIATELLA

SERVES

6 cups chicken stock (page 20)
3 skinless, boneless chicken
   breast halves, cut into strips
4 eggs
$2/3$ cup freshly grated
   Parmesan cheese
large handful of fresh parsley,
   minced
black pepper

The important thing with this soup is to take it off the heat as soon as you have added the egg mixture, or it will overcook. The egg, Parmesan and parsley will float to the top like a raft, leaving the rich broth and chunks of chicken beneath. If you don't want to make your own stock you can use canned chicken bouillon, or even bouillon powder or a cube.

Place a saucepan over high heat, pour in the stock and bring to a boil. Add the chicken strips and cook for 5 minutes.

Meanwhile, in a small bowl, beat the eggs with the cheese, minced parsley and black pepper.

Pour the egg mixture into the boiling liquid, then immediately remove from the heat. Divide the soup among six large bowls and serve with good bread and butter or olive oil.

CHICKEN AND ASPARAGUS CHOWDER

SERVES

7 tbsp butter
1 large onion, roughly chopped
2 large celery stalks, roughly
  chopped
1 garlic clove, roughly chopped
1 lb (450 g) asparagus, roughly
  chopped
1 bay leaf
²/₃ cup all-purpose flour
8 cups chicken stock (page 20)
2 cooked chicken breast
  halves, skinned and meat
  shredded
¹/₄ cup heavy cream
salt and white pepper

Melt the butter in a large saucepan. Add the onion and celery with some salt and pepper. Cook for 5 minutes without coloring. Add the garlic and asparagus and cook for 2 minutes longer. Season again, then add the bay leaf and flour and stir well. Continue cooking for 2 minutes, stirring often.

Pour in the stock, stir and bring to a boil. Skim off any funny bits and give the bottom of the pan a good scraping. Simmer for 15 minutes, then take the pan off the heat. Discard the bay leaf. Transfer the soup to a food processor and blend until smooth.

Return the soup to the saucepan and bring to a boil. Taste and season as you like. Drop in the shredded chicken and heat through. Remove from the heat, stir in the cream and serve.

Variation: you can replace the asparagus with 3 cups of canned or thawed frozen corn kernels, well drained.

SQUASH AND CHICKEN SOUP WITH BEAN SPROUTS AND CILANTRO

SERVES

6 tbsp red curry paste

$^1/_3$ cup palm sugar

1 butternut squash, peeled and cut into 1$^1/_2$-inch (3.8 cm) chunks

2 cans (14 oz/400 g each) coconut milk

$^3/_4$ cup coconut cream

1 tbsp Thai fish sauce

2 tbsp lime relish

3 lemongrass stalks, crushed

4 skinless, boneless chicken breast halves, cut into strips or chunks

1 lb (450 g) precooked mung-bean noodles or egg noodles

1 heaped cup fresh bean sprouts

leaves from a small bunch of cilantro

FRIED GARNISH

1$^1/_4$ cups vegetable oil

$^1/_3$ cup thinly sliced fresh chilies

$^1/_3$ cup thinly sliced garlic

$^1/_2$ cup thinly sliced shallots

Adding lime relish was a last-minute thing when I first made this dish. I wanted a little more piquancy and spice. Normally I wouldn't add an Indian flavor to a Thai recipe, but it worked perfectly. The result is fragrant, sweet, sour, hot and salty, with all these flavors taken up by the noodles. The fried garnish is optional.

For the garnish, heat the oil in a wok and add the chilies. Cook slowly over low heat until all the moisture from the chilies has evaporated (at which point the oil will stop bubbling). Then raise the heat slightly so that they caramelize and crisp up, without turning too dark. Remove the chilies with a slotted spoon and repeat the process with the garlic, followed by the shallots. Set them all aside.

Drain off all but 5 tablespoons or so of the oil from the wok. Add the red curry paste to the wok and fry for 2 minutes, then add the palm sugar and let it cook with the curry paste until sticky and fragrant, about 4 minutes. Add the butternut squash, stir well and cook for 2–3 minutes.

Pour in the coconut milk and coconut cream, then add the fish sauce, lime relish and lemongrass. Bring to a boil and cook over medium heat until the squash is soft but not mushy, 20–30 minutes. Add the chicken, bring back to a boil and cook for 5 minutes but no longer.

Put the precooked noodles in a bowl and pour boiling water over them. Leave for 2 minutes to reheat, then drain. Divide the noodles among serving bowls and add a few pieces of squash per portion. Ladle in the soup and garnish with the fried chilies, garlic and shallots, plus the bean sprouts and cilantro.

CHICKEN SOUP
WITH COCONUT MILK

SERVES

small bunch of cilantro,
   ideally with roots
   (coriander root)
4 small, fresh green chilies
2 stalks lemongrass
8 oz (225 g) skinless, boneless
   chicken breast, cut into
   slices lengthwise
4 cups thin coconut milk
1 cup thick coconut milk
8 thick slices galangal, peeled
10 Kaffir lime leaves, torn
1/4 cup fish sauce
1/4 cup lime juice

Coconuts grow in abundance in the south of Thailand, and the milk extracted from their flesh is used for everything. This soup (called *tom kha gai*) is just one example. Because coconut milk is naturally sweet, the soup can be quite spicy — as the number of chilies indicates. This serves four as a first course, or six to eight as part of a full Thai meal.

Separate the cilantro leaves from the stems. Set the leaves aside for the garnish, and crush the roots and stems together in a mortar with a pestle. Remove the cilantro, then crush the chilies in the mortar. Bruise the lemongrass with the flat side of a knife, then cut it into 1-inch (2.5 cm) pieces.

In a large saucepan, combine the chicken, thin coconut milk, lemongrass, galangal and crushed cilantro roots and stems. Bring to a boil and simmer for 4 minutes.

Add the lime leaves and chilies, then stir in the thick coconut milk. Bring back to a boil. Immediately take the pan off the heat and add the fish sauce and lime juice. Taste and correct the seasoning, if necessary. Serve the soup garnished with the reserved cilantro leaves.

CHICKEN AND GALANGAL SOUP

SERVES

8 oz (225 g) skinless, boneless chicken breast, cut into fine strips

5 thick slices galangal

2 stalks lemongrass, bruised and cut into 1-inch (2.5 cm) pieces

3 cilantro (coriander) roots, bruised

6 small, fresh green chilies, crushed in a mortar

2 large, fresh red chilies, deseeded and cut into small pieces

3 tbsp fish sauce

3 Kaffir lime leaves, torn

¼ cup lime juice

10 fresh Thai basil leaves

Although similar to the famous Thai soup *tom yum*, this simple recipe has a more delicate flavor, which is the result of cooking the chicken in water. Stock would be too strong here, its flavor overpowering. Cilantro and coriander are different names for the same herb. Look for it with roots in Asian or Latin markets, where it might be identified as coriander root. The soup serves four as a first course, or six to eight when served as part of a full Thai meal.

Put the chicken in a large saucepan and cover with 4 cups of cold water. Bring to a boil and add the galangal, lemongrass, cilantro roots and all the chilies. Simmer for 4 minutes.

Add the fish sauce and lime leaves, then taste and adjust the seasoning, as necessary. Remove the saucepan from the heat and add the lime juice and Thai basil leaves just before serving.

YUGOSLAVIAN CHICKEN SOUP WITH SPAETZLE

SERVES

1 whole chicken
2 potatoes
3 parsnips
2 onions
a lot of parsley stems, plus
 a large handful of chopped
 fresh parsley leaves
salt and pepper

SPAETZLE
²/₃ cup all-purpose flour
pinch of salt
1 egg
1 tbsp warm milk

Spaetzle are a type of noodle or dumpling. To make them it is helpful to have a special spaetzle maker, which is like a metal tray with holes drilled in it. Alternatively, you can use a pastry bag fitted with a small nozzle to make the little worm shapes.

Yugoslavians tend to thicken their soups by including lots of potato in the broth, which makes the spaetzle a bit unnecessary, in my opinion. So I use far less potato than some may say is authentic.

Put the chicken in a big pot, cover with water, add a large handful of salt and place over the heat. After 20 minutes pour off the water and throw it away.

Peel and finely dice the potatoes, parsnips and onions. Add them to the pot with the parsley stems, some salt and pepper and enough fresh water to cover. Bring to a boil, then reduce the heat and simmer gently for 5–6 hours.

Lift out the chicken. Strain the stock and skim off the fat. Cut the breast meat from the chicken and shred it (keep the rest of the chicken for other dishes). Put half the stock in a saucepan with the breast meat, and the remaining stock in another large saucepan for cooking the spaetzle.

Mix all the spaetzle ingredients together to form a thick batter. Bring the reserved stock to a boil. Push the batter through a spaetzle maker (or squeeze it through a pastry bag fitted with a small nozzle, cutting it into matchstick lengths) into the boiling stock. They take about 2 minutes to cook. Lift them out with a slotted spoon and plunge them into cool water.

Reheat the soup, then add the parsley leaves and the spaetzle. Stir well and serve.

GAME CONSOMMÉ WITH GAME DUMPLINGS

SERVES

CONSOMMÉ
1 carrot, peeled and cut into
  chunks
1 celery stalk, cut into chunks
1 shallot, cut into chunks
a few sprigs of fresh parsley
1/2 cup ground chicken
1 cup ground pork
2 egg whites
4 ice cubes, crushed
8 cups game stock (page 21),
  plus 1 3/4 cups extra for
  cooking the dumplings
salt and pepper

DUMPLINGS
2 oz (55 g) chicken, duck or
  other poultry livers
1 1/3 cups all-purpose flour
2 oz (55 g) finely chopped beef
  suet (from a butcher)

GARNISH
4 boneless pheasant breast
  halves
vegetable oil
handful of fresh chervil leaves
truffle oil

I like this deep-flavored, livery soup. The dumplings are delicious and add that richness that the game deserves. Consommé needs great stock — this is one of those times when you really should make your own.

To make the consommé, put the carrot, celery, shallot, parsley and some salt and pepper in a food processor and blend until the vegetables are minced. Add the ground meats, egg whites and ice, and process again.

In a large pot, stir the stock and meat mixture together. Set over low heat and cook gently until the meat mixture floats to the top to form a raft. Increase the heat and let simmer gently for 30 minutes — do not boil. Remove from the heat and set the consommé aside, without stirring it.

To make the dumplings, put the livers, flour, suet and a little salt and pepper in a food processor. Blend until smooth. Roll the resulting dough into hazelnut-sized balls and chill to firm.

Preheat the oven to 350°F (175°C). In a wide saucepan, bring the extra stock to a simmer. Drop the dumplings into the stock and cook for 20 minutes, then drain. Meanwhile, set an ovenproof frying pan over medium-high heat. Rub the pheasant breasts generously with vegetable oil and seasoning, then sear in the hot frying pan, giving plenty of color to the skin and underside. Transfer to the oven to cook for 15 minutes.

Remove the pheasant from the oven and let it rest for 5 minutes, then slice thickly. Meanwhile, strain the consommé gently and slowly, preferably through cheesecloth. Reheat if necessary. Put some dumplings in each serving bowl, ladle in the consommé and garnish with chervil and a few drops of truffle oil. Serve with the sliced pheasant alongside.

GAME BROTH
WITH PEARL BARLEY

SERVES

1 large onion
1 large carrot
1 turnip
2 small partridges
3¼ cups game stock (page 21)
1 tbsp pearl barley
large handful of chopped
   fresh parsley
flaky sea salt and pepper

Here is a good hearty, wintry soup that is a meal all on its own. It is best in my opinion to make it a few days before you want to eat it — the flavor just gets better and better.

Peel the vegetables and cut them into dice about the size of your little fingernail. Take the breasts and legs off the partridges.

Put the partridge legs, stock and diced vegetables in a heavy-based ovenproof casserole over medium heat and bring to a simmer. Add the pearl barley and adjust the heat so that the liquid barely simmers (if it boils, the vegetables will break up). Let cook, uncovered, for 20 minutes.

Preheat the oven to 350°F (175°C). Lay the partridge breasts on top of the soup and transfer to the oven to cook for 1 hour.

Remove the casserole from the oven. Lift out the legs and strip the meat from the bones, chopping it very finely. Cut the breast meat into small dice. Return all the meat to the soup and season to taste (a heaped teaspoon of sea salt and a good amount of pepper would be my advice). Stir in the parsley just before serving, and eat with hot bread.

CHINESE DUCK SOUP WITH NOODLES

SERVES

1 Chinese roast duck (page 174)

1 carrot, peeled and roughly
  chopped

1 celery stalk, roughly chopped

1 large onion, roughly chopped

1 leek, roughly chopped

2-inch (5 cm) piece fresh
  ginger, peeled and sliced

6 star anise

1/2 tsp black peppercorns

large bunch of cilantro, ideally
  with roots (coriander root)

2 tbsp toasted sesame oil

3 tbsp fish sauce

8 green onions, thinly sliced

1 lb (450 g) cooked egg noodles

sliced fresh chilies, to taste
  (optional)

If you don't want to prepare your own Chinese roast duck, you might be able to buy Chinese-style roasted duck in a supermarket. Alternatively, ask your local Chinese restaurant to sell you a whole Peking duck.

Remove the legs and breasts from the duck and cut into portions, then either slice or shred the meat, whichever you prefer.

Chop the duck carcass into four or five pieces and put them in a pot. Cover with about 4 quarts (16 cups) of water and bring to a boil. Skim any fat from the surface, then turn the heat down to a simmer and add the carrot, celery, onion, leek, ginger, star anise and peppercorns. Simmer until the stock has reduced by half, 1–2 hours, skimming the surface regularly.

Meanwhile, wash and dry the cilantro. Pick the leaves and set aside. Chop the stems and roots, keeping them separate from the leaves.

When the stock has reduced, strain it through a fine sieve into a clean saucepan. Bring back to a boil, then lower the heat to a simmer. Add the sesame oil and fish sauce and stir. Crush the cilantro stems and roots, add them to the soup and simmer for 20 minutes longer.

Just before serving, add the green onions, noodles and chilies (if using). Divide the duck and noodles among serving bowls, then ladle the soup over the top. Scatter on the cilantro leaves and serve immediately.

Little dishes, little plates of deliciousness that surprise with huge flavors, that have no real rule as to when they should be eaten or how they should be eaten — these are the things that you'll find in this chapter.

Has the world of eating changed, or is it just my own personal preference to eat dishes from virtually anywhere in the world all at the same time? For me, not being restricted to one cuisine is exciting and makes a meal far more enjoyable. Small dishes, bits and pieces that get plonked on the table or handed around, are the way forward when it comes to impressing not just your friends but your taste buds.

I have always loved the vibrancy of Asia, and many of the dishes here have been influenced by my travels in Thailand, as well as styles of cooking that have stayed with me from growing up in Australia, where Indonesia and Thailand are our neighbors. I've also included a true childhood favorite, one that I still hold in high regard: the great chicken and stuffing sandwich. Brilliant in its simplicity, it is comforting in winter and satisfying in summer — even when packed for a beach picnic and the added crunch of sand has somehow made it into the mix.

snacks and appetizers

EGG ROLLS WITH CHICKEN AND SHRIMP

MAKES

2 oz (55 g) vermicelli noodles
2 garlic cloves
1 cilantro (coriander) root
5 white peppercorns
pinch of salt
1 tbsp vegetable oil, plus
  6 cups for deep-frying
2 oz (55 g) shelled raw shrimp,
  ground (about ¼ cup)
¼ cup ground chicken
2 tbsp fish sauce
1 tbsp palm sugar
1 heaped cup bean sprouts,
  ends trimmed
2 tbsp cilantro leaves
2 tbsp sliced Chinese shallots
15 egg-roll wrappers
¼ cup all-purpose flour
sweet chili sauce, for serving

Egg-roll wrappers or skins can be found in Asian markets and many supermarkets. Any that you don't need for this recipe can be wrapped in plastic wrap and kept in the freezer for another day.

Soak the noodles in warm water for at least 10 minutes, then drain and cut into ¾-inch (2 cm) pieces with scissors. Meanwhile, pound together the garlic, cilantro root, peppercorns and salt in a mortar to make a fine paste, or blend in a food processor.

In a wok, heat 1 tablespoon of oil over medium heat and fry the garlic paste until fragrant. Add the ground shrimp and chicken, and fry until cooked, about 3 minutes. Add the noodles, followed by the fish sauce and palm sugar. Transfer the mixture to a bowl and let cool.

Mix the bean sprouts, cilantro leaves and shallots into the cooled shrimp mixture. To make each roll, place an egg-roll wrapper on a board and place 1 tablespoon of the filling along the center. Fold up the bottom edge of the wrapper, then fold over the left and right sides. Roll up the wrapper almost to the top. Mix the flour with 2 tablespoons of water and use a bit of this paste to seal the top edge. Repeat with the rest of the ingredients.

Heat the oil for deep-frying to 425°F (220°C). Working in batches of six or so, deep-fry the egg rolls for about 3 minutes, turning them over toward the end of the cooking time so that they are evenly browned. Drain on paper towels and let cool a little before serving with sweet chili sauce.

CHICKEN IN SCREWPINE LEAF

MAKES

1³/₄ lb (800 g) chicken meat
  with skin, ground
4 tsp Thai oyster sauce
1 tbsp black bean sauce
1 green onion, chopped
2 garlic cloves, sliced and
  deep-fried
12 screwpine (pandan) leaves
vegetable oil for deep-frying

In Thailand, this dish is mainly cooked on the street rather than in restaurants and is usually made with cubes of chicken soaked in red vinegar and soy. A Thai lady showed me this version using ground chicken. The screwpine leaves impart a smoky flavor when deep-fried, but don't try to eat them.

In a bowl, mix together all the ingredients except the screwpine leaves and oil for deep-frying. Divide the chicken mixture into 12 portions and roll into balls.

Clean and flatten the screwpine leaves. Hold one leaf with the pointed end to the sky. Place a chicken ball 1½ inches (3.8 cm) from the base, then fold the base up over the chicken. Twist the remaining leaf around the chicken ball to wrap it completely. Push the pointed tip of the leaf under the first layer and pull it through tightly to secure.

Heat the oil for deep-frying in a wok or deep pan. Grasp the stuffed leaves in a bunch, holding them by the pointed ends, and gently lower into the hot oil. Fry until the chicken mixture is cooked through, 7–8 minutes, and serve immediately.

SALT-AND-PEPPER LEMON CHICKEN

SERVES

4 cups vegetable oil
10 white peppercorns
2 heaped tbsp coarse sea salt
²/₃ cup all-purpose flour
grated zest of 1 lemon
1 lb (450 g) boneless chicken
 thighs
mayonnaise, soy sauce or
 sweet chili sauce, for serving

Slowly heat the vegetable oil in a wok or deep pan. Meanwhile, pound the peppercorns and sea salt together in a mortar, then tip into a shallow bowl and stir in the flour and lemon zest. Preheat the oven to 350°F (175°C) and put a baking sheet in it to heat at the same time.

When the oil starts to shimmer it is ready for cooking. Toss the chicken in the seasoned flour until well coated. Add about a quarter of the chicken pieces to the hot oil and fry for 4–5 minutes. When the chicken is done it should float to the top of the oil, curl and turn crisp.

Remove the chicken from the oil and place on the hot baking sheet in the oven while you fry the remainder in batches. Serve with little bowls of mayonnaise, soy sauce or sweet chili sauce.

PORTUGUESE CHICKEN CROQUETTES

MAKES

2 chicken breast halves, about
   7 oz (200 g) each
4 tbsp butter
1 tbsp chopped onion
3 tbsp all-purpose flour, plus
   extra for coating
1 cup milk
1 cup chopped cooked ham
1 tbsp English mustard powder
1 tbsp chopped fresh parsley
2 eggs, beaten
2 cups dry bread crumbs, for
   coating
4 cups vegetable oil
salt and pepper

These are wonderfully addictive — once you have started eating them it's hard to stop. They will stay hot for at least 10 minutes so make brilliant little party snacks. You could also make them with turkey.

Poach the chicken in enough simmering salted water to cover for 10 minutes, then let cool in the liquid (you can also use chicken leftover from a roast). Once cool, drain and discard all the skin and bones. Put the cooked chicken in a food processor and blend to a smooth paste.

Heat the butter in a saucepan and fry the onion until soft. Add the flour and cook, stirring constantly, until it begins to brown. Gradually add the milk and continue cooking and stirring for 10 minutes. Stir in the chicken, ham, mustard and parsley. Add some salt and pepper and mix well. Let the mixture cool a little; it will become a thick paste.

Shape the mixture into small sausage shapes. Dust all over with flour, dip in the beaten eggs, and then coat with the bread crumbs, pressing them on really well. Put the croquettes on a tray and refrigerate for at least an hour to set them.

When ready to cook, heat the oil in a wok or deep pot. When it starts to shimmer, drop in a few croquettes and deep-fry until they are golden and float to the top of the oil, 4–5 minutes. Drain the cooked croquettes on paper towels and keep them warm while you cook the rest in batches.

Let the croquettes cool a little before serving, because if you bite into them right away they will burn your mouth.

ROAST CHICKEN AND
STUFFING SANDWICH

SERVES

lots of soft butter
2 big, thick slices white bread
mayonnaise
cold or hot roast chicken,
  stripped from the bone
cold, or maybe even hot,
  stuffing or dressing
handful of arugula

Butter the bread, then spread lots of mayonnaise over one of the slices. Pile the chicken on the mayonnaise and then the stuffing. Add some arugula. Cover with the other slice of bread and press down before cutting the sandwich in half.

Also good with: watercress 🐓 pea shoots 🐓 coleslaw
🐓 baby romaine 🐓 iceberg

GRILLED CHICKEN WITH GUACAMOLE

SERVES 🐔🐔🐔🐔🐔🐔🐔🐔🐔🐓🐓

6 skinless, boneless chicken
  breast halves
olive oil
corn chips, for serving
salt and pepper

GUACAMOLE
1¼ cups cubed plum or Roma
  tomatoes
1 small red onion, diced
8 fresh basil leaves
large handful of fresh parsley,
  leaves picked from stems
1 fresh red chili (mild or hot,
  to taste), finely diced
2 tbsp olive oil
½ tsp Tabasco sauce, or
  to taste
2 limes, halved
2 avocados
large bunch of cilantro

Grill the chicken breasts following the method on page 62, then set aside.

To make the guacamole, put the tomatoes and onion in a mixing bowl. Roughly chop the basil and parsley leaves and add to the bowl along with a large pinch of salt and a grind of pepper. Add the chili, olive oil, Tabasco and a generous squeeze of lime.

Peel the avocados, remove the pit and cut the flesh into hunks. Place in a bowl and squeeze the juice from one of the limes over the avocado. Drain off 2 tablespoons of the juice that has come out of the tomatoes and add to the avocado. Mix with a fork until it becomes a chunky mash. Chop half the cilantro and add it along with the tomato-onion mixture.

Slice or shred the chicken and serve it with the corn chips and guacamole, garnished with the rest of the cilantro. You might want to put a jar of mayo and some cold beers on the table, too.

DEVILED CHICKEN LIVER CROSTINI

MAKES

10 chicken livers, cleaned and fat removed

4 sage leaves, fresh or preserved in salt, plus 16 fresh sage leaves for garnish (optional)

4 juniper berries

4 tbsp olive oil

1 garlic clove, peeled but left whole

$^1/_2$ cup dry red wine

16 pieces Tuscan bread or other rustic bread, about 3 inches (7.5 cm) square and $^1/_4$ inch (0.6 cm) thick

salt and pepper

Preheat the oven to 400°F (200°C). Finely chop five of the chicken livers along with four of the sage leaves and the juniper berries.

Heat the oil in a small, heavy saucepan over medium heat. Add the chopped ingredients and the garlic and sauté for 10 minutes. Pour in the wine and let it bubble away for 10 minutes.

Put the bread on a baking sheet and warm up in the oven for 10 minutes. Meanwhile, cut the remaining chicken livers into quarters and add them to the saucepan. Season with a bit of salt and pepper and cook for 4 minutes. Remove the pan from the heat and transfer the contents to a bowl.

Spread a tablespoon of the chicken liver mix over each piece of bread. Arrange the crostini on a large serving platter, and if fresh sage is available place one leaf on top of each crostini to garnish.

BREADED CHICKEN LIVERS WITH BÉARNAISE

SERVES 🐔 🐔 🐔 🐔 🐔 🐔

2/3 cup all-purpose flour
2 eggs
a little milk
2 cups fine, dry bread crumbs
24 chicken livers
2 cups vegetable oil
salt and pepper

BÉARNAISE SAUCE
7 tbsp white wine vinegar
1 shallot, chopped
a few sprigs of fresh tarragon
2 egg yolks
1/2 cup warm melted butter

It is important to cook these little morsels fairly slowly so that the crumbs stay beautifully golden and crisp while the livers cook through to be pink in the center.

Put the flour in a bowl and season well with salt and pepper. Beat the eggs and milk together in a bowl and set it next to the flour. Line up the bread crumbs in a third bowl. Working one or two at a time, roll the livers in the flour, then dip them in the egg and lift out, letting the excess egg drain off. Finally, roll the livers in the bread crumbs, patting them on firmly and making sure they are thoroughly coated. Set aside in a cool place.

To make the sauce, put the vinegar, shallot and tarragon in a saucepan and boil until the mixture has reduced by about three-quarters. Let cool, then pour into a large stainless-steel bowl. Set the bowl over a pan of barely simmering water. Add the egg yolks and whisk until the mixture is thick enough so that you can see the whisk leaving a pattern. Remove the bowl from the pan and slowly add the melted butter, whisking all the time. Season to taste and keep warm.

Preheat the oven to 300°F (150°C). Put a large, heavy frying pan containing half of the oil over medium heat. Once hot, lay six to eight livers in the pan — they should sizzle a little. Cook for a minute or so on each side until golden but not dark brown; adjust the heat as necessary. Put the cooked livers on a baking sheet in the oven to keep warm while you fry the remainder in fresh oil. Serve hot with the béarnaise sauce.

CHOPPED LIVER AND ONIONS

SERVES 🐔 🐔 🐔 🐔 🐔 🐔

$^1/_2$ cup schmaltz, ground

10 oz (285 g) chicken livers

2 cups finely diced onions

3 hard-boiled eggs, peeled and
chopped

handful of chopped fresh
parsley

rye bread and pickled
gherkins, for serving

salt and pepper

**The important part here is the schmaltz — that is,
the chicken fat from inside the cavity of the raw bird,
which is very good indeed. If you don't have any you
can use a little vegetable oil instead.**

Heat the schmaltz in a frying pan until it melts. Add the livers
and onions and cook for 15 minutes, stirring constantly. Season
with some salt and pepper during cooking. Remove from the heat
and let cool for 5 minutes.

Tip the contents of the pan onto a chopping board and, with a big
knife in each hand, chop the mixture like mad as though you
were mincing it. About halfway through the chopping add the
eggs, then continue chopping until the mixture is almost a paste.

Serve with chopped parsley, rye bread and gherkins.

CHINESE DUCK PANCAKES (PEKING DUCK)

SERVES

1 large Chinese roast duck
 (page 174)
20 thin Chinese pancakes
 (Peking doilies)
sliced cucumber
sliced green onions
hoisin sauce

If your roast duck is cold, reheat it in a preheated 425°F (220°C) oven for 40 minutes. Meanwhile, steam the Chinese pancakes over hot water, and get the other accompaniments ready on separate plates.

Take the duck from the oven and shred the meat with two forks. Serve with the pancakes, cucumber, green onions and hoisin sauce, letting everyone create their own wraps at the table.

EGGPLANT AND MISO PICKLE

SERVES

vegetable oil, for deep-frying
3 large eggplants
3/4 cup red miso
1/2 heaped cup sugar
1/2 cup chicken stock (page 20)
4 green onions, cut at an angle
1 heaped tbsp togarashi or
 hot chili powder

DRESSING
1/2 cup light soy sauce
3 1/2 tbsp sugar
1 cup plus 1 tbsp rice vinegar
2 tbsp sake
1–2 fresh red chilies, minced
3 tbsp peanut oil

Another great way to serve Chinese roast duck.

Heat oil in a deep-fryer to 425°F (220°C). Meanwhile, cut the eggplants into 3/4-inch (2 cm) cubes. When the oil is hot, fry the cubes until golden brown; drain on paper towels.

In a saucepan, heat the miso, sugar and stock for a few minutes. Add the fried eggplant and cook until soft. Add the green onions and chili powder and remove from the heat.

To make the dressing, combine the soy sauce, sugar, vinegar, sake and chilies in a small bowl. Blend in the peanut oil. Serve the Chinese roast duck on the eggplant pickle with the dressing spooned over the top.

TURKEY AND WILD MUSHROOMS ON TOAST

SERVES

14 oz (400 g) skinless, boneless
   turkey breast, cut into small
   cubes (about 2 heaped cups)
4 tbsp butter
3 tbsp olive oil
splash of brandy (optional)
1 large shallot, diced
7 oz (200 g) mixed wild
   mushrooms
4 thick slices bread
2 tbsp crème fraîche
salt and pepper

Season the diced turkey with salt and pepper. In a heavy frying pan, melt 3 tablespoons of the butter with 2 tablespoons of the olive oil, then drop in the turkey. Sauté, stirring, until cooked through, about 10 minutes. Add a splash of brandy, if you want the dish to be more grown-up. Remove the turkey from the pan and set aside.

Add the remaining butter and oil to the pan and cook the shallot until it starts to color, about 3 minutes. Add the mushrooms and season well with salt and pepper. Cook for 4 minutes, then turn the mushrooms over and cook for 2 minutes longer. Meanwhile, toast the bread.

Return the turkey to the pan and add the crème fraîche. Bring just to a boil, then remove the pan from the heat and spoon the turkey and mushroom sauce over the toast.

TURKEY AND CORN FRITTERS

SERVES

3½ cups all-purpose flour
2 tbsp baking powder
2 tsp salt
2 tsp paprika
1 tsp sugar
2 eggs
about 1 cup milk
5 cups roughly chopped
  cooked turkey
1¼ cups canned or frozen corn
  kernels, drained if necessary
4 green onions, sliced
handful of chopped cilantro
handful of chopped fresh
  parsley
vegetable oil, for frying

FOR SERVING
tomato chutney or relish
6 big handfuls of arugula
¾ cup sour cream
olive oil, for drizzling
salt and pepper

I like diner-style food and one of my very favorite places to sit and watch the world go by while chowing down is New York's Union Square Diner. They serve huge plates of food like this and it's all delicious.

Preheat the oven to 400°F (200°C). Sift the flour, baking powder, salt and paprika into a large bowl. Stir in the sugar and make a well in the center. In a separate bowl, beat the eggs and milk together. Gradually add them to the well in the dry ingredients, whisking until you have a smooth, stiff batter.

Combine the turkey, corn, green onions and herbs in a mixing bowl. Add just enough batter to bind them lightly together. Heat a little oil in two large, nonstick frying pans, then ladle in about 2 tablespoons of batter per fritter. Cook until golden brown on both sides. Put the cooked fritters on a baking sheet and put them into the oven while you cook the remaining fritters.

To serve, place a fritter on each plate and top with a spoonful of tomato chutney, some arugula leaves and then a spoonful of sour cream. Set another fritter on top, like a sandwich. Finish with a little olive oil and a sprinkling of salt and pepper.

PAN-GRILLED QUAIL WITH SPICED LENTILS

SERVES

LENTILS

7 tbsp olive oil, plus extra-
virgin olive oil for drizzling
2 red onions, finely chopped
1 leek, finely chopped
1 carrot, finely chopped
3 garlic cloves, crushed
handful of fresh thyme leaves
a few fresh sage leaves,
chopped
2 cups Puy lentils (French
green lentils)
5 tomatoes
3 green onions, chopped
dash of red wine vinegar
handful of cilantro
handful of fresh flat-leaf
parsley, chopped

BOUQUET GARNI

1 carrot, halved lengthwise
1 leek
sprig of fresh sage
3 sprigs of fresh thyme
1 celery stalk, halved
lengthwise

QUAIL

16 boned quail (page 59)
a little olive oil
salt and pepper

Quail has sweeter meat than chicken. The birds are small, but the eating is easy if the bones are taken out, and licking your fingers at some stage is mandatory.

Start with the lentils. Heat the olive oil in a heavy pan and gently sweat the onions, leek and carrot with the garlic, thyme and sage until the vegetables are just soft. Add the lentils.

Make the bouquet garni by tying the carrot, leek, sage, thyme and celery in a bundle with kitchen string. Add to the pot of lentils. Pour in enough water to cover the lentils, plus a little more, then cook at a gentle simmer for about 30 minutes (don't boil the love out of them, as the Italians say!).

Add the tomatoes and continue simmering very gently until the lentils are soft but still a bit firm, about 30 minutes. (You will need to replenish the water every now and then.) The finished lentils should have a slightly soupy consistency.

Heat a ridged, cast-iron grill pan. Season the quail and rub with oil. When the pan is hot, place the quail in it skin-side down and cook for 2 minutes, then turn them over and cook for 2 more minutes. Repeat so the total cooking time is 8 minutes.

While the quail are cooking, add the green onions to the lentils, season well and cook for 10 minutes. Stir in the vinegar and cilantro, and finish with the parsley and extra-virgin oil. Serve the quail on the lentils.

SALT-AND-PEPPER QUAIL
WITH SWEET CHILI SAUCE

SERVES

4 cups vegetable oil
10 white peppercorns
2 heaped tbsp coarse sea salt
²/₃ cup all-purpose flour
4–5 garlic cloves
6 boned quail (see opposite)
large handful of cilantro,
   leaves picked from stems

CHILI DRESSING
3 dried chilies, toasted and
   deseeded
¹/₃ cup palm sugar
juice of 2 limes
¹/₂ cup fish sauce

To make the dressing, pound the roasted dried chilies in a mortar with a pestle. Add the palm sugar and continue pounding, adding the lime juice and fish sauce. Set aside.

Preheat the oven to 350°F (175°C) and put a baking sheet in it to heat up at the same time. Meanwhile, slowly heat the vegetable oil in a wok or deep-fryer. Pound the peppercorns and sea salt together in a clean mortar, then add the flour and set aside.

Peel half the garlic and pound it with the remaining whole cloves (the cloves should split open and the flesh and skin should come together). Throw the pounded garlic into the hot oil, lower the heat to a bubble and let cook for 5 minutes, stirring every so often. When done, the garlic will float to the top and be crisp. Lift out the garlic with a strainer and drain well on paper towels.

Reheat the oil: when it starts to shimmer it is ready. Toss the quail in the seasoned flour so that they are well coated. Drop three quail into the oil and fry until crisp, 4–5 minutes. Remove from the oil and place on the hot baking sheet in the oven to keep warm while you cook the remaining quail.

Put the fried garlic and cilantro leaves in a large bowl and add a smidgen of the chili dressing. Toss well. Pile onto individual plates, set the quail on top and spoon the dressing around the outside

CRISP-FRIED QUAIL AND MUSTARD GREENS

SERVES 🐔🐔🐔🐔🐔🐔🐔🐔🐔🐔

1/2 bunch of green onions, finely diced

4 tbsp soy sauce, plus extra for garnish

10 boned quail (see below)

2 quarts (8 cups) vegetable oil, plus 4 tbsp for stir-frying

3/4 cup potato flour

2 1/2 tbsp five-spice powder

scant 1 oz (30 g) fresh ginger, peeled and cut into julienne

1 lb (450 g) Chinese mustard greens, split lengthwise

2 tbsp yellow bean paste

3 1/2 tbsp oyster sauce

The day before serving, combine the green onions and soy sauce in a big bowl. Add the quail. Let marinate for 24 hours, if possible.

Heat the oil in a deep-fryer to 425°F (220°C). Mix together the potato flour and five-spice powder. Remove the quail from the marinade and pat on the flour mixture without draining them too much. Working in batches of three or four, place the quail in the hot oil and fry for about 4 minutes. Drain on paper towels and keep in a warm oven while you deep-fry the rest.

Heat a wok with 4 tbsp of vegetable oil. Add the ginger followed by the mustard leaves and yellow bean paste and cook, stirring, for about 3 minutes. Remove from the heat and add the oyster sauce. Cover the wok and let the greens braise in its warmth for about 10 minutes.

You can serve the quail and greens on individual plates with dabs of soy sauce around the sides, but I like to pile them up on a large platter in the middle of the table and let people help themselves.

HOW TO BONE QUAIL

Use scissors to cut down each side of the quail's backbone and lift it out. Hold the bird in both hands and push the breast with your thumbs, applying pressure to the rib cage and the breast-plate. Set the splayed bird on a board, skin-side down, so you can see the bones and ease them away with your fingers. Use a small knife to take out the thighbone by slipping the knife under the bone and cutting it out.

Ah, that age-old question: leg or breast? It still divides the world, but I reckon there is a time for the breast and there is a time for the leg. The difference is quite simple — one is soft and sweet but needs time and nurturing (the leg), the other is lean and quick to cook (the breast) but needs something else with it to really bring it to life, to bring out its beauty.

A chicken breast has become a favorite regular supper for many people. Simply pan-grilled or grilled over hot coals, the skin should be crisp and the meat tender and moist. On its own, though, it isn't enough. You can add whatever you want as a side, from fries and mayo to more sophisticated and spicy accompaniments like harissa and stewed chickpeas. Fill the breast with garlic butter and protect it with crumbs, then fry, and you have the great chicken Kiev. The breasts of other fowl are just as versatile.

I have to admit, though, that I love the legs of all kinds of poultry. So a dish that presents both the breasts and the legs, in separate pieces so you can choose your favorite, is the best for me.

legs and breasts

GRILLING CHICKEN

When chicken is grilled it's often cooked to death — dry and nasty — or it's charred outside and raw in the center. The right heat is the secret, along with leaving the skin on to protect the soft, white meat. The chicken will be cooked properly if you just let it grill slowly, either in a grill pan or over grayish-red coals.

I realize that most people prefer chicken breasts, but for me the flavor of the meat and skin on the legs is far, far better. You can cook them just as easily if you buy leg parts (or just thighs) that have been boned. Don't try to grill them with the bones still in — the result will be tough.

To pan-grill, heat a ridged cast-iron grill pan until it is hot, then turn the heat down. Season the chicken with salt and just a little bit of pepper, and rub oil all over it. Gently lay the chicken skin-side down in the pan and let it sizzle for 4–5 minutes. Then turn it over and give it just a few minutes on the other side. Turn it back onto the skin side again and add a couple of pieces of butter and some more salt. Repeat the process, with 4–5 minutes on the skin side and a few more minutes on the other side.

The rules for grilling chicken breasts and legs over coals are a bit different. The fat dripping from the skin can cause flare-ups, so do not rub oil all over, just on the meat side. Place the chicken skin-side down over the hot coals and cook for 5 minutes, then put the barbecue cover on and cook for 3 minutes longer. Turn the chicken over and put a little butter (or flavored butter) on top of each piece so it melts into the skin. Put the cover back over the barbecue and let cook for 3 more minutes. Check to be sure that the coals aren't too hot (no flames) and if necessary take the cover off. Then let the chicken cook for a final 5 minutes or so. Take the chicken from the barbecue and let it rest for a couple of minutes, then slice and serve.

FRIES AND MAYO

Using a frying basket, fry the potatoes in three batches so the oil reheats quickly and browns the fries nicely.

6 large potatoes, peeled and cut into thickish
  1¼-inch (3 cm) sticks
5 quarts (20 cups) corn or vegetable oil
salt
½ cup mayonnaise
4 lemon wedges
4 handfuls of watercress

Soak the potatoes in cold water for 5 minutes, then change the water and let soak for another 5 minutes. Meanwhile, heat the oil to 254°F (120°C) in a deep-fryer. Drain the potatoes and pat them dry with paper towels.

Fry each batch for 8–10 minutes, then drain well and leave on a tray to cool.

Heat the oil again to 375°F (190°C). Still working in batches, fry the potatoes for 2 minutes. Give them a little shake in the basket, then continue frying until well colored, 4–5 minutes longer. Drain the fries on paper towels for a few minutes before sprinkling them with salt. Serve with the chicken, plus mayo, lemon wedges and watercress. SERVES 4.

PANZANELLA

This salad is best after a bit of rough and tumble: it needs to be worked together so all the flavors blend.

7 tbsp red or white wine vinegar
a big bowl of leftover bread, cut into
  thumb-sized chunks
6 ripe tomatoes, roughly chopped
1 red onion, chopped
large handful of chopped fresh flat-leaf parsley
chopped olives and sweet peppers (optional)
⅓ cup pine nuts, toasted
about 3 tbsp John's vinaigrette (page 101)

Mix the vinegar with 7 tablespoons water. Pour over the bread and stir so the bread soaks up the liquid. Squeeze the bread to get rid of the excess liquid and set aside.

Put the tomatoes in a large bowl, giving half of them a squeeze. Add the onion and parsley and stir, then add the bread and mix well. Add the rest of the ingredients and stir again. Leave for at least 20 minutes while you cook the chicken, then serve together. SERVES 6.

GINGER CHICKPEAS AND HARISSA

3 tbsp vegetable oil
2 tsp garam masala
4 oz (110 g) fresh ginger, peeled and minced
1 fresh red chili, deseeded and minced
14 oz (400 g) can chickpeas, drained
14 oz (400 g) can crushed tomatoes
large handful of cilantro leaves, coarsely
  chopped
lemon wedges or halves
4 heaped tbsp harissa
salt and pepper

Heat the oil in a saucepan until smoking. Add the garam masala and sizzle for 30 seconds, then add the ginger and chili and stir well. Add the chickpeas and stir to coat them in the spices, then add the tomatoes, a large pinch of salt and a good grind of pepper. Bring to a boil. Remove from the heat and stir in the cilantro.

Serve with the chicken, with the lemon and a dollop of harissa on the side. SERVES 4.

POMEGRANATE, SPINACH AND OLIVE SALAD

The crisp skin of the chicken and its tender meat, the crunchy pomegranate seeds and olives, and iron-rich spinach combine beautifully in this simple salad.

1 pomegranate, halved
24 large green olives, sliced
juice of 1 lemon
2 tbsp olive oil
2 handfuls of baby spinach leaves
salt and pepper

Scoop the seeds from the pomegranate and mix them in a bowl with the sliced olives, lemon juice and olive oil. Let sit for 20 minutes while you cook the chicken.

Shred the spinach and season it with salt and pepper.

To serve, chop or slice the cooked chicken, put it on serving plates and scatter the salad ingredients over the top. SERVES 4.

THAI CUCUMBER SALAD

$^1/_3$ cup palm sugar
4 tbsp fish sauce
1 cup coconut milk
$^1/_2$ cucumber, halved and deseeded
2 small shallots (the little Thai ones, if possible),
 very thinly sliced
$^1/_2$ small red pepper, deseeded and cut into thin strips
2 fresh, long red chilies, deseeded and cut into
 thin strips
large handful of cilantro leaves
4 Kaffir lime leaves, torn (optional)
handful of fresh Thai basil leaves
$^2/_3$ cup roasted peanuts, chopped

Combine the palm sugar, fish sauce and coconut milk
in a heavy frying pan. Bring to a boil, then simmer for
10 minutes. Set aside to cool.

Use a vegetable peeler to cut the cucumber into long,
thin strips and put them in a bowl with the shallots,
pepper and chilies. Pour the cooled dressing over the
vegetables and let stand for 10–15 minutes. Stir in the
herbs and sprinkle the nuts over the top. SERVES 6.

SALSA VERDE AND MASH

Traditionally served with boiled meats, salsa verde
(green sauce) is delicious with chicken as well as pork
and fish. Make it in advance of serving if you wish — it
will keep for few days in the refrigerator. Serve the
chicken and sauce with mashed potatoes, following my
recipe on page 157.

handful of fresh flat-leaf parsley
handful of fresh basil
2 garlic cloves, crushed
1 hard-boiled egg
handful of fresh white bread crumbs
1 tbsp white wine vinegar
1 tbsp capers, drained
$3^1/_2$ tbsp olive oil
pinch of salt

Put the parsley, basil and crushed garlic in a food
processor and blend to a paste. Add all the remaining
ingredients and continue processing for 2 minutes.
SERVES 4.

SEA-SPICED EGGPLANT

2 medium eggplants, cut into $^1/_2$-inch (1.2 cm) strips
$^1/_2$ cup vegetable oil
1-inch (2.5 cm) piece of fresh ginger, peeled and cut
 into matchsticks
4 green onions, thinly sliced at an angle
3 fresh red chilies, deseeded and thinly sliced
4 tbsp oyster sauce
1 tbsp fish sauce
2 tbsp cilantro leaves

Put the eggplant strips in a wok, cover with cold water
and bring to a boil. Drain and cool, then pat dry.

Dry the wok and place it over high heat. Add the oil
and then the ginger and eggplant. Cook until the
eggplant is evenly browned, 5–6 minutes (avoid stirring
too much as this will make it mushy). Stir in the chilies
and three-quarters of the green onions.

Drain off most of the oil, then return the wok to the
heat. Stir in the oyster and fish sauces and cook for a
final 2 minutes before adding the remaining green
onions and cilantro. SERVES 4.

HUMMUS AND PAPRIKA

2 heaped cups freshly cooked chickpeas (cooking
 liquid reserved)
3 tbsp tahini
4 garlic cloves
juice of 4 lemons
7 tbsp olive oil, plus extra for serving
salt and white pepper
paprika, for sprinkling

While the chickpeas are still hot, put them in a food
processor with the tahini and garlic. Blend to a paste.
Add half the lemon juice, half the oil and 1 teaspoon
salt. Turn on the machine again and, as the mixture
starts to thicken, add a little of the cooking liquid and
then some more lemon juice and oil.

Keep adding these liquids until the hummus is like a
thick sauce (it will thicken more as it cools). Adjust the
seasoning, adding more lemon and oil if desired.

To serve, swirl the hummus over the plates, add the
grilled chicken, sprinkle with paprika and drizzle on
some extra olive oil. SERVES 4.

CHICKEN KIEV

SERVES

4 tbsp butter, softened
1–2 fat garlic cloves, minced
2 tbsp chopped fresh parsley
1/2 tsp finely grated lemon zest
2 tsp lemon juice
2 skinless chicken supremes
  (breast halves with wing
  bone left on)
3–4 tbsp all-purpose flour
1 tsp paprika
1 extra-large egg
1 cup dry bread crumbs
sunflower oil, for frying
flaky sea salt and pepper

FOR SERVING
mashed potatoes (page 157)
wilted spinach

Who could not love chicken Kiev? Sweet, tender chicken crusted with crisp crumbs, and herb-rich butter flowing from the center. That describes the perfect chicken Kiev and this is the perfect recipe.

To make the filling, mix together the butter, garlic, parsley, lemon zest and juice, and some salt and pepper. Shape into two logs and chill until firm but not solid.

Preheat the oven to 375°F (190°C). Make a slit lengthwise in each chicken breast and open it out like a book. Lay each flat between two pieces of plastic wrap with the bone pointing away from you and bash with a meat pounder or rolling pin until about 1/4 inch (0.6 cm) thick. Place a log of butter on each flattened breast, 3/4 inch (2 cm) in from the edge, then roll up the chicken and secure with wooden toothpicks.

Mix the flour, paprika and some salt and pepper together in a shallow bowl. Beat the egg in another shallow bowl. Toss the stuffed chicken breasts in the flour until coated; shake off any excess. Slide the chicken into the beaten egg and turn until covered. Repeat to cover with flour and egg once more. Finally, dip into the bread crumbs and turn to coat completely.

Pour oil into a medium frying pan to a depth of about 1/2 inch (1.2 cm) and heat thoroughly. Toss in a small cube of bread to check the temperature — it should sizzle and brown right away. Lower the chicken breasts carefully into the pan and spoon some of the hot oil over the top for about 1 minute to seal the crumbs. Turn over to brown the other side, again spooning oil over the top until the crust is golden — this should take 1–2 minutes longer.

Transfer the chicken to a shallow roasting pan and bake until the breasts feel firm when pressed, 12–14 minutes. Remove and drain on paper towels. Carefully remove the toothpicks and serve with mashed potatoes and spinach.

CHICKEN WITH TARRAGON SAUCE

SERVES

olive oil
2 chicken breast halves
salt and pepper

TARRAGON SAUCE
$\frac{1}{2}$ cup brandy
$\frac{1}{2}$ cup crème fraîche
handful of chopped fresh
  parsley
handful of torn fresh tarragon
  leaves

Although we've shown this with mashed potatoes in the picture, it's just as nice with French fries.

Heat a heavy frying pan over medium heat and add a little olive oil. Season the chicken well and place it skin-side down in the pan. Cook for 8 minutes, then turn the breasts over and cook for the same time again. Check to see if the chicken is cooked through, then remove it from the pan and keep warm.

Raise the heat under the pan to very high. Add the brandy and carefully flame it to burn off the harsh taste of alcohol. Shake or stir to incorporate the pan juices and sticky bits from the bottom of the pan. Stir in the crème fraîche, then taste and season. Bring the sauce to a boil and reduce by half. Add most of the parsley and tarragon leaves.

Serve the sauce with the chicken, pouring the brown juices that come from the rested chicken over the dish as well. Sprinkle with the last of the chopped herbs.

SOUTHERN-FRIED CHICKEN

SERVES 🐓🐓🐓🐓🐓🐓

1 whole chicken, cut into
  8 pieces
1½ tsp salt
1⅓ cups all-purpose flour
1 tsp ground white pepper
2 tsp cayenne pepper
2 tsp paprika
2 tsp ground allspice
2 tsp ground thyme
6 cups vegetable oil, for frying
2 eggs, beaten

FOR SERVING
gravy (page 156)
lemon wedges
mayonnaise

Give this a whirl and you will never buy takeout again. Well, you might, but it won't be as good as this!

Score the skin of the chicken pieces, then place them in a large bowl of cold water. Add a heaped teaspoon of salt. Let soak for 2 hours.

Mix together all the dry ingredients, including the remaining ½ teaspoon of salt, and set to one side. Take the chicken from the water and pat it dry with paper towels. Drop the chicken into the flour mixture and toss to coat each piece well. Set aside for 10–15 minutes.

In a deep-fryer, heat the oil to 425°F (220°C). At the same time, heat the oven to 350°F (175°C). Set a wire rack inside a roasting pan and put into the oven to heat.

Coat the chicken pieces in the beaten egg, then drop them into the seasoned flour again. When the oil has reached frying temperature, put two or three pieces in the pan and deep-fry for 6–8 minutes. Remove them to a tray. Bring the oil back to the correct temperature and continue frying the chicken.

Arrange all the fried chicken on the rack in the hot pan and return to the oven. Bake until cooked through, about 20 minutes. Cut open a piece to check for doneness: the chicken should not be pink near the bone. Serve hot with some gravy, wedges of lemon and mayo.

TURKEY ESCALOPE CORDON BLEU

SERVES

4 thin slices turkey breast
  (cutlets), about 8 oz
  (225 g) each
4 slices cooked ham
4 slices Emmental cheese
vegetable oil, for frying

GARLIC-HERB BUTTER
3–4 tbsp chopped fresh
  flat-leaf parsley
3–4 tbsp chopped fresh chives
1 tsp chopped fresh tarragon
1/2 cup unsalted butter,
  softened
2 garlic cloves
1/2 tsp English mustard powder
salt and pepper

FOR BREADING
1/3 cup all-purpose flour
2 eggs, beaten
2–3 cups fresh bread crumbs

An oldie but a goodie.

Start with the garlic-herb butter. Put the herbs and softened butter in a bowl. Crush the garlic cloves with a little salt until you have a smooth paste, then add to the butter mixture. Add the mustard and some pepper and mix well. Divide the butter into four little logs, wrap in plastic wrap and chill to harden.

Put each piece of turkey between two sheets of plastic wrap and bash with a meat pounder or rolling pin until they are very thin and about the size of a small plate. Lay the cutlets on a board, smooth-side down, and season with pepper. Lay a slice of ham on each and then a slice of cheese. Unwrap the flavored butter, place a piece in the middle of each cutlet, and fold up like an envelope.

Line up the flour, beaten eggs and bread crumbs in three separate shallow dishes. Dip each turkey parcel into the flour, making sure it is well coated, then dip into the eggs and finally the crumbs, making sure at each stage that it is well coated. Put the parcels on a tray and chill for 30 minutes before cooking.

Heat the oven to 350°F (175°C). When ready to cook, heat the oil in a large frying pan. Add the turkey parcels and cook for 2 minutes on each side. Transfer the parcels to the hot oven to continue cooking until golden, about 5 minutes. Remove the turkey parcels from the oven and drain on paper towels before serving.

SCHNITZELS

SERVES

⅓ cup all-purpose flour
2 eggs, beaten with a little milk
2 cups fine, dry bread crumbs
4 skinless, boneless chicken
  thighs, bashed out to about
  the size of your hand
vegetable oil, for frying
salt and pepper

It is important to cook these fairly quickly so that the meat remains succulent while the crumbs become beautifully golden and crisp. You could serve them with lemon wedges and pickles, or in a big bun with lettuce, tomato or beet slices, and mayonnaise.

Heat the oven to 300°F (150°C). Put the flour in a bowl and season well with salt and pepper. Put the bowl of beaten egg mixture next in line, and a bowl of bread crumbs last. Roll the chicken cutlets in the flour, then dip into the egg, letting the excess drain back into the bowl as you lift them out. Next, roll the chicken in the bread crumbs, patting on firmly and making sure they are well coated all over. (You may find it easiest to coat all the chicken cutlets in the flour, then all of them in the egg, and then all in the crumbs.)

Heat a wide, heavy frying pan, then add 2 tablespoons of oil. Once the oil is hot, slide in two schnitzels (assuming they fit, of course). They should sizzle a little. Cook until they are golden (not dark) brown, about 4 minutes on each side. Lower or increase the heat as necessary.

Transfer the schnitzels to the oven to keep warm while you cook the remainder. Add more oil if the pan is a bit dry, but let it get hot before you add the schnitzels.

DUCK BREASTS

There is a great secret to cooking the perfect duck breast — with a crisp skin and succulent meat that is pink in the center — and that secret is to start with a cold frying pan and no oil. It's true.

Take four duck breasts; don't trim them. Lay them meat-side down on a board and use your knife to score the skin all the way through to the meat, without cutting into it. Make sure you score all the way to the edge of the breast so that as the skin shrinks during cooking it doesn't pull the meat in and make it tough. Season the skin (and only the skin) with a generous amount of salt and ground black pepper.

Lay the duck skin-side down in a cold, heavy frying pan. Set the pan over medium heat. Now just wait. Do not move the pan or move the duck. What is going to happen over the next 10 minutes is that the fat under the skin will slowly melt and the skin will become brown and crisp.

When the skin starts to color around the outside you are ready to move on. By now the pan should have ½–¾ inch (1.2–2 cm) of duck fat in it and all the fat from the breast should have melted. Season the meat side now, then turn the duck breasts over and cook for 2 minutes. Increase the heat to high for just 1 more minute of cooking. Take the pan from the heat and leave the breasts in the pan for 5 minutes while you finish off your side dishes, then slice and it will be very sexy indeed.

You can keep the rendered duck fat for cooking roast potatoes: simply drain it into a heatproof glass bowl and refrigerate. Four duck breasts will produce just under 1 cup of duck fat. You may find some brown "jelly" at the bottom of the bowl, which is just concentrated duck stock.

ROASTED PUMPKIN AND PINE NUTS

4¹/₂-lb (2 kg) piece pumpkin, or 1 butternut squash,
  peeled and deseeded
3 tbsp olive oil
a little fresh oregano
¹/₃ cup pine nuts, toasted
2 tbsp John's vinaigrette (page 101)
lemon halves or wedges, for serving
flaky sea salt and pepper

Heat the oven to 400°F (200°C). Cut the pumpkin or
squash into 1¹/₂-inch (3.8 cm) chunks and toss with the
oil and seasoning in a roasting pan. Roast until tender,
about 50 minutes.

Mix the pumpkin or squash with the oregano and
pine nuts in a large bowl. Spoon the dressing over the
top and mix well but gently. Serve with the duck plus
some lemon to squeeze over. SERVES 4.

BOK CHOY AND CHILI

2 tbsp vegetable oil
2 garlic cloves, chopped
6 small heads bok choy, halved lengthwise
3 tbsp oyster sauce
2 tbsp light soy sauce
1 fresh red chili, finely sliced

Heat the oil in a wok. Add the garlic and stir-fry for
2 minutes. Add the bok choy and continue stir-frying
until it wilts, about 2 minutes. Pour in the oyster and
soy sauces and add 3 tablespoons of water. Cook for
1 minute longer, then sprinkle with the chili and toss
together. Serve with the duck. SERVES 6.

ZUCCHINI FRITTERS

1¹/₃ cups all-purpose flour
2 tsp baking powder
1 tsp paprika
3 eggs
about ¹/₂ cup milk
2 large zucchini, grated
olive oil, for frying
a little sour cream (optional)
mustard, for serving
salt and pepper

Sift the flour, baking powder, paprika and a large pinch
of salt into a large bowl, then make a well in the center.
In a separate bowl, whisk together the eggs and milk.
Add the egg mixture to the dry ingredients and whisk
until you have a smooth, stiff batter. Mix in the grated
zucchini.

Heat a little oil in a nonstick frying pan. Drop in a
ladleful of batter per fritter and cook until golden
brown on both sides. Sprinkle the cooked fritters with
a little olive oil, salt and pepper, plus a dollop of sour
cream if desired, then serve with the duck breasts and
your favorite mustard. SERVES 4.

CELERY-ROOT MASH

10 oz (285 g) celery root (also called celeriac),
  peeled and cubed
¹/₂ cup milk
¹/₂ cup olive oil, plus extra for drizzling
¹/₂ cup water mixed with a little lemon juice
chopped fresh parsley
salt and pepper

Put the celery root in a saucepan with the milk, olive oil
and enough lemon water to cover. Season, then bring to
a boil and cook over low heat until tender, about 20
minutes. Test the celery root with a fork to make sure it
is soft. Drain, reserving the cooking liquid. Roughly
mash the celery root with a fork. Mix in some parsley
and a little of the cooking liquid to give a soft
consistency. Drizzle a little olive oil over the top and
serve with the duck. SERVES 2.

WILD MUSHROOMS AND NEW POTATOES

1 lb (450 g) small new potatoes
2 tsp olive oil
2 garlic cloves
1 fennel bulb, cut into eighths
2 bay leaves
2 sprigs of fresh thyme
7 oz (200 g) mixed wild mushrooms, cleaned
some dried morels
1/2 cup white wine
salt and pepper

Parboil the potatoes for 10 minutes, then drain and peel when cool.

Preheat the oven to 350°F (175°C). Heat the oil in an ovenproof casserole. Add the garlic and a grind of black pepper, then add the potatoes, fennel, bay leaves and thyme, and stir. Cook until the potatoes are just starting to color, about 4 minutes.

Add the mushrooms and dried morels and cook for 10 minutes over high heat, stirring occasionally. Add the white wine, bring to a boil and boil for 30 seconds, then cover and cook for about 2 minutes.

Transfer the casserole to the hot oven to finish cooking, about 15 minutes. Season well and serve hot with the duck. SERVES 6.

SKORDALIA

1 lb (450 g) potatoes, peeled and cubed
5 garlic cloves
1/2 cup milk
1/2 cup olive oil, plus extra for drizzling
juice of 1 lemon, plus lemon halves or wedges
    for serving
salt and white pepper

Put the potatoes in a heavy saucepan with the garlic, milk, olive oil and some seasoning and set over medium heat. Bring to a boil and cook until the potatoes are soft, 15–20 minutes.

Remove from the heat, and drain off and reserve the cooking liquid. Blend the potatoes in a food processor with the lemon juice and half the cooking liquid. Return the skordalia to the saucepan and reheat. Drizzle a little olive oil over the skordalia, then serve alongside the duck, with lemon halves or wedges to squeeze over. SERVES 2.

CRUSHED PEAS AND MINT

4 cups frozen green peas
handful of fresh mint, stems and leaves separated
3 green onions, chopped
4 tbsp salted butter
1/2 cup heavy cream
olive oil, for drizzling (optional)
lemon halves or wedges, for serving

Put the frozen peas in a medium saucepan with the mint stems. Pour in 1/2 cup of boiling water and set over high heat. Add the green onions and butter. Bring to a boil and cook for 3 minutes. Add the cream and bring back to a boil.

Remove the pan from the heat and, using an immersion blender (or a food processor), blend the pea mixture until coarse-fine. Chop the mint leaves and add them to the crushed peas as you gently reheat them. Spoon onto each serving plate, top with the duck and add a drizzle of olive oil, if desired. Serve with lemon. SERVES 4.

OLIVES AND BABY ONIONS

The idea of gigantic salty olives with sweet little onions, a hint of chili, and a good splash of sherry vinegar to get the digestion of that rich duck going, is for me a real beauty of a dish.

2 tsp butter
4 oz (110 g) boiling onions, peeled
1 heaped cup large purple and green olives, pits
    removed and flesh squashed
1/2 tsp dried red pepper flakes
2 tbsp sherry vinegar

Melt the butter in a heavy saucepan. Add the onions, turn the heat down low and cook gently for 10 minutes; don't let them brown. Add the olives and pepper flakes and stir well. Increase the heat a bit and cook for 5 minutes. Add the vinegar, turn the heat up and boil for a minute or so. Serve with the duck. SERVES 4.

SQUAB WITH BACON AND CORN FRITTERS

SERVES

3 squabs
olive oil
12 slices bacon
about ½ cup sour cream
salt and pepper

CORN FRITTERS
1⅓ cups all-purpose flour
2 tsp baking powder
1 tsp paprika
3 eggs
about ½ cup milk
1¼ cups canned corn kernels,
  drained
2 green onions, sliced
handful of chopped cilantro
handful of chopped fresh
  parsley

To make the corn fritters, sift the flour, baking powder, paprika and a large pinch of salt into a large bowl. Make a well in the center. In a separate bowl, combine the eggs and milk. Gradually add the egg mixture to the dry ingredients and whisk until you have a smooth, stiff batter. Add the corn, green onions and herbs. Set aside.

Preheat the oven to 350°F (175°C). Rub the squabs with oil and season well with salt and pepper. Set a heavy ovenproof frying pan over medium heat. When the pan is hot, add 1 or 2 tablespoons of oil. Lay the squabs on their sides in the frying pan. Let them color well, then turn onto the other side. Once that is colored, turn onto their backs and color that. Transfer the pan to the oven. After 3 minutes give the pan a little shuffle, then cook for a few more minutes (the meat will be very pink at this point). Remove the squabs and let them rest while you make the fritters. Turn the oven to very low.

Heat a little oil in a nonstick frying pan. Cooking two or three at a time, make six fritters, frying them until golden brown on each side. As the fritters cook, put them on a baking sheet and keep warm in the oven. While the fritters are cooking, fry the bacon in a separate pan and keep it warm in the oven, too.

Carve the breasts from the squabs. To assemble the dish, place a corn fritter on each serving plate and top with two slices of bacon and a squab breast. Spoon some sour cream over the top and sprinkle with a little olive oil and some salt and pepper.

PHEASANT WITH CABBAGE ROLLS

SERVES 🐓🐓🐓🐓🐓🐓🐓🐓

4 pheasants
olive oil
salt and black pepper

SAUCE
2 tbsp butter
1/2 cup chopped shallots
1/3 cup chopped garlic
2/3 cup sliced mushrooms
1/2 cup sherry vinegar
1 cup dry sherry
2 cups chicken or game stock
   (pages 20–21), plus about
   1 1/4 cups extra

CABBAGE ROLLS
1 head savoy cabbage
1/2 cup ground veal or pork
2 large shallots, chopped
1/3 cup cooked white rice
handful of chopped fresh
   parsley

Start with the sauce. Melt half the butter in a small saucepan and sweat the shallots, garlic and mushrooms until soft and golden. Deglaze the pan with the vinegar, letting it reduce to a syrupy consistency. Add the dry sherry, and when it is very hot carefully set it alight. Keep boiling until the volume of liquid has reduced by half. Add the stock and reduce on a lower heat, skimming often, until the sauce is a light *jus*. Season to taste, then strain through a fine sieve into a clean pan. Set aside.

While the sauce is reducing, make the cabbage rolls. Pull off eight good outer leaves from the cabbage. Finely slice the rest of the cabbage. Bring a pot of salted water to a boil and blanch the sliced cabbage for 1 minute; drain and refresh under running cold water. Next, blanch and refresh the big cabbage leaves, then let them drain on a dish towel. Remove the central vein if it is fibrous and thick.

Preheat the oven to 350°F (175°C). In a large mixing bowl, combine the sliced cabbage, ground meat, shallots, rice, parsley and some salt and pepper, mixing with your hands. Place an egg-sized pile of filling on the stem end of each cabbage leaf. Fold up the end and sides, then roll into a cigar shape, making sure no filling can escape. Put the cabbage rolls in a baking dish and pour in enough stock to come three-quarters of the way up the sides of the rolls. Braise in the oven for 30–40 minutes.

Meanwhile, heat a large, heavy ovenproof frying pan. Rub the pheasants with oil and seasoning, then place in the hot pan and color all over. Transfer to the oven and roast for 15 minutes. Let rest slightly before carving.

Reheat the sauce. It should have a light coating consistency, so reduce it further if necessary. Just before serving whisk in the remaining butter. To serve, place a pheasant breast and leg on each plate along with two of the cabbage rolls and coat with 2 or 3 tablespoons of the sauce.

A good salad must be fresh. It must be balanced: It needs bits of crisp and crunchy, and bits of soft and succulent. It needs the acid of an unctuous dressing and the sweetness and fragrance of soft herbs. The meat for your salad — be it freshly poached or grilled, or cold leftovers from a roast — is best shredded or torn rather than neatly cut.

A salad is really fork food, relaxed food. You do all the work in the composition: the chopping and slicing, poaching or roasting, mixing the dressing or cooking the sauce. Then it's all done and ready to plop in a bowl — a handful of this and a handful of that and then a delicate stir.

It doesn't matter whether you like your salad served in a big bowl or as a single pretty little plate. Just take the time to organize and get all those bits ready.

Otherwise, there are no rules for salads. Many of the dressing recipes here make more than you need for one salad, but I think that if something will keep, you should make plenty of it. You'll find plenty of ways to use it up over the next few days.

salads

HOW TO POACH A CHICKEN

1 carrot
1 onion
1 leek
1 celery stalk
1 chicken, about 2¹/₂ lb (1.1 kg)
2 bay leaves
small bunch of fresh parsley
¹/₂ tsp black peppercorns

I usually use roast chicken for salads, but if you prefer poached chicken, here's how to do it perfectly.

Cut the vegetables into biggish pieces and put in a pot with the chicken, bay leaves, parsley, peppercorns and just enough water to cover. Poach gently for 40 minutes, then remove from the heat and let the bird cool in the liquid.

Once cool, lift the chicken from the pot and use as desired. Strain the stock and use it for other dishes.

CHICKEN, CRAB AND AVOCADO SALAD

SERVES

7 oz (200 g) plum or Roma
  tomatoes, deseeded and
  cubed (about 1½ cups)
1 small red onion, finely diced
8 fresh basil leaves, roughly
  chopped
2 tbsp roughly chopped fresh
  parsley leaves
1 tbsp olive oil
½ tsp Tabasco sauce
1 tbsp balsamic vinegar
2 cups shredded roast or
  poached chicken
1 cup packed fresh white
  crabmeat
2 avocados
4 lemons, halved
handful of cilantro leaves
salt and pepper

The sweetness of crab and tomatoes goes well with the shredded roast chicken, punchy dressing and rich avocado in this salad.

Put the tomatoes, onion, basil and parsley in a mixing bowl with a large pinch of salt and a grind of pepper. Add the olive oil, Tabasco and balsamic vinegar and set aside.

Mix the chicken with the crabmeat and set aside (this can be kept in the refrigerator for a few hours if need be).

Peel the avocados and remove the pits. Mash the flesh with a fork, then squeeze on the juice from one of the lemons. Drain off 2 tablespoons of dressing from the tomatoes and add it to the avocado.

To serve, place a few large spoonfuls of tomato salad on each plate. Top with some of the chicken and crabmeat and then the avocado. Garnish with cilantro leaves and sit the lemon halves on the side of the plate.

CHICKEN WITH COCONUT DRESSING

SERVES

⅓ cup palm sugar

3½ tbsp fish sauce

14 oz (400 g) can coconut milk

6 skinless, boneless chicken thighs

2 red Thai shallots

½ red pepper, cut into julienne

2 small, fresh red chillies, cut into julienne

2 oz (55 g) cucumber, cut into julienne (about ⅓ cup)

1 heaped tbsp roasted peanuts

4 Kaffir lime leaves, cut into very fine julienne

30 cilantro leaves

6 squares banana leaf, for serving (optional)

Combine the palm sugar, fish sauce and coconut milk in a large saucepan and bring to a boil. Add the chicken and poach until cooked through. Let cool.

Mix the other ingredients (except the banana leaves) together in a bowl.

When the chicken is cool, cut it into strips that are ½ inch (1.2 cm) thick. Toss into the salad.

Lay a banana leaf on the center of each plate and pile the salad on top. Drizzle some of the poaching liquid over and serve.

CHICKEN LARP

SERVES

2 cups finely ground chicken
2 tbsp fish sauce
6 tbsp lime juice
8 red Thai shallots, sliced
4 tbsp fresh mint leaves
4 tbsp cilantro leaves, plus
   cilantro sprigs for garnish
4 tbsp roasted rice powder
   (page 98)
1 tbsp hot chili powder
   (ground hot chili pepper),
   toasted
finely shredded fresh chilies
salt

This fiery dish will burn your mouth, but I love it — as hot as I can take it. Adjust the quantity of chili powder and shredded fresh chilies to your taste.

Simmer the chicken in a pan with a little salted water until cooked, about 3 minutes, stirring often. Remove from the heat and let cool to room temperature.

Just before serving, add the fish sauce, lime juice, shallots, mint and cilantro leaves, and roasted rice and chili powders. Taste for seasoning: the flavor should be hot, salty and sour. If necessary, add a few extra drops of lime juice to sharpen and define the flavor. Serve sprinkled with shredded chilies and cilantro sprigs.

CHICKEN CAESAR SALAD

SERVES

7 tbsp vegetable oil

4 oz (110 g) pancetta or bacon, cut into small strips

2 thick slices white bread or ½ baguette

2 cups freshly grated Parmesan cheese, plus 2¼ oz (65 g) Parmesan cheese, shaved

4 heads baby romaine, leaves separated, or 1 large head romaine, leaves torn into large pieces

4 large chicken breast halves, grilled (page 62) and sliced

2 oz (55 g) can anchovy fillets, cut in half lengthwise

black pepper

DRESSING

1 egg plus 1 egg yolk

1 tbsp Dijon mustard

1 tbsp shallot vinegar

2 anchovy fillets, minced

1 garlic clove, crushed

1 cup vegetable oil

1 cup olive oil

I think there is something irresistible about crisp lettuce, very well chilled, covered in a creamy dressing. The recipe here makes more dressing than needed, but it will keep in the refrigerator for a few days. Do bear in mind, though, that it contains raw egg. Anchovies should be included in a classic Caesar salad, but if you don't want them that is fine. Just add a little salt.

Heat the vegetable oil in a heavy frying pan, add the pancetta and fry gently over medium heat, moving them constantly so they don't stick or burn. When crisp, remove from the pan with a slotted spoon and drain on paper towels.

Cut the bread into ½-inch (1.2 cm) cubes and add to the oil in the pan. Fry for a few minutes until golden brown on all sides, then remove with a slotted spoon and drain on paper towels. While the croutons are still warm, tip them into a bowl and sprinkle with 1–2 tablespoons of the grated Parmesan.

To make the dressing, whisk together the egg, egg yolk, mustard, vinegar, anchovies and garlic in a large bowl until the mixture begins to thicken and turn pale. Slowly add the oils, whisking constantly, until well amalgamated. Add a little hot water if the mixture seems too thick. Stir in the rest of the grated Parmesan.

To serve, place the lettuce leaves in a bowl and toss with enough of the dressing to coat thoroughly. Scatter the croutons, pancetta, chicken and anchovy fillets over the leaves and finish with the shaved Parmesan and a grinding of black pepper.

SMOKED CHICKEN COB SALAD, MY STYLE

SERVES 🐓🐓🐓🐓🐓🐓🐓🐓

7 oz (200 g) cooked, peeled
  beets
2 heaped tbsp red-currant jelly
1½ tbsp red wine vinegar
6 canned palm hearts, halved
  lengthwise or sliced
2 heads romaine, leaves
  separated
1¼ cups canned corn kernels,
  rinsed and drained
3 slices bacon, cooked and
  crumbled
7 oz (200 g) crumbly blue
  cheese, such as Stilton
14 oz (400 g) smoked chicken,
  thinly sliced
4 hard-boiled eggs, quartered
4 tbsp Caesar dressing
  (page 94)
flaky sea salt and pepper

Cut the beets into quarters and place in a saucepan with the red-currant jelly and vinegar. Bring to a boil and cook until the beets are well coated with a sticky sauce, about 10 minutes. Set aside to cool.

Divide the palm hearts and lettuce among eight serving plates. Arrange the beets on top of the leaves and sprinkle with the corn and bacon bits. Crumble the blue cheese roughly into ¾-inch (2 cm) pieces and place on top. Add the sliced smoked chicken and then a couple of egg quarters per plate. It will look a bit messy, but that is the idea. Sprinkle with some salt and pepper and drizzle the Caesar dressing over just before serving.

CORONATION CHICKEN CUPS

MAKES

2 roast or poached chickens,
   cooled
3 tbsp good-quality curry
   powder, or the equivalent
   in curry paste
2 cups mayonnaise
1 cup heavy cream
$^2/_3$ cup raisins
4 heads baby romaine
handful of chervil leaves,
   for garnish

Strip the meat off the chickens, discarding all cartilage, bones and skin. Tear the meat into small finger-sized pieces and put into a large bowl.

In another bowl, mix the curry powder or paste with the mayonnaise, then stir in the cream and raisins. Pour this dressing over the chicken and fold together thoroughly.

Pull apart the heads of romaine until you have 24 good-sized leaves. Arrange these lettuce "cups" on a large platter and spoon some of the chicken mixture into each one. Garnish with chervil and serve. To eat, pick up a lettuce cup, wrap the lettuce around the filling, and bite.

SPICED DUCK SALAD, THAI HERBS AND ROASTED RICE

SERVES

DUCK
4 duck legs
3 tbsp fish sauce
4-inch (10 cm) piece of
  galangal, bashed
3 lemongrass stalks, bashed
11 Kaffir lime leaves
½ cup coconut milk

SALAD
½ cup Thai jasmine rice
2 green papayas or 4 Thai
  green mangoes, peeled and
  cut into julienne
¼ cup finely chopped snake
  beans (Chinese long beans)
  or string beans
⅓ cup thinly sliced napa
  cabbage
4 fresh red chilies (e.g.
  serranos), deseeded and
  minced
bunch of fresh Thai basil

DRESSING
1 fresh red Thai chili
1 fresh green Thai chili
2 tbsp fish sauce
2 tbsp lime juice
1 tbsp palm sugar
1 tbsp granulated sugar
1 tbsp tamarind water
  (page 114)

You only need a little roasted rice to add crunch to this recipe, but it is worth roasting a jar full and keeping it to add to any salad. I prefer to cut the papaya in strips rather than pound it, as is traditional in Thailand.

The day before serving, rub the duck all over with the fish sauce, then leave, skin-side down, in this marinade for 12 hours or so.

Next day, preheat the oven to 425°F (220°C). Put the rice in a bowl, cover with water and let soak for 5 minutes; drain. Scatter the rice over a baking sheet and roast until the grains turn off-white in color, begin to pop, and develop a nutty fragrance, about 30 minutes. Transfer to a bowl to cool, then grind the roasted rice to a powder and store in a jar.

To cook the duck, shake off the excess fish sauce and place the legs in a baking dish with the galangal, lemongrass and three of the lime leaves. Pour the coconut milk over the top. Place in the oven to cook for about 2 hours. Turn the oven down to 350°F (175°C) and continue cooking until the duck meat will fall away from the bone easily, about 1 hour.

Remove the duck from the oven. Lift off the skin and lay it on a rack in a roasting pan. Return it to the oven and cook until it is crisp and dry, about 30 minutes. Crumble and reserve.

In a large bowl, combine the papaya, beans, cabbage, chilies, basil, a handful of roasted rice and the remaining lime leaves, which should be cut into thin strips. Shred the duck meat and add to the bowl.

For the dressing, crush the chilies in a mortar, then add the remaining ingredients and pound until smooth. Pour the dressing over the salad and toss to coat. Serve immediately, before the vegetables start to go limp.

DUCK WITH POMELO, WATERMELON AND CASHEWS

SERVES

4 duck legs, cooked and
  shredded (see page 98)
½ daikon
1 pomelo
7 oz (200 g) watermelon
  flesh, cut into chunks
  (about 2 cups)
⅔ cup cashews
3 green onions, cut into strips
1 carrot, shredded
large handful of cilantro,
  leaves picked from stems
large handful of fresh Thai
  basil, leaves picked from
  stems
4 heads baby romaine
20 fresh chives, for tying

DRESSING
1 fresh red Thai chili
1 fresh green Thai chili
2 tbsp palm sugar
2 tbsp fish sauce
2 tbsp lime juice
1 tbsp tamarind water
  (page 114)

If you have not already done so, cook the duck legs and shred the meat.

To make the dressing, crush the chilies in a mortar, then add the palm sugar and pound to a paste. Stir in the fish sauce, lime juice and tamarind water and continue to pound until the dressing is well mixed. Set aside.

Use a mandoline or a vegetable peeler to shred the daikon into paper-thin strips approximately 2½ inches (6.3 cm) long. Peel the pomelo, then take the segments between your fingers and rub them so that the flesh breaks into small pieces.

In a mixing bowl, combine the daikon, pomelo, watermelon, cashews, green onions, carrot, and cilantro and basil leaves.

Peel the leaves from the heads of lettuce until you get to the hearts; reserve the leaves. Shred the hearts and add them to the salad bowl along with the duck meat. Stir the dressing into the salad and let sit for 2 minutes so the vegetables wilt slightly.

Take the lettuce leaves and place a good spoonful of salad in the center of each one. Bring in the sides, then roll up to make a parcel. Tie with a chive stalk. Alternatively, put everything out on the table and let people roll their own.

GOOSE, APPLE AND WATERCRESS SALAD

SERVES

2 Granny Smith apples
10 oz (285 g) roast goose meat,
    cooled and thinly sliced
4 handfuls of watercress, large
    stems removed
handful of fresh flat-leaf
    parsley, leaves picked from
    stems
large handful of toasted
    walnuts

JOHN'S VINAIGRETTE
    (MAKES 1¾ CUPS)
1 tbsp Dijon mustard
5 tbsp red wine vinegar
1 tsp walnut oil
1¼ cups olive oil
flaky sea salt and pepper

This works a treat: sour apples, peppery watercress and a simple but punchy vinaigrette. It is very easy to make and a perfect foil for leftover goose, which is sometimes a difficult meat to use up.

To make the dressing, whisk the mustard and vinegar in a bowl until blended. Slowly add the oils, still whisking, then season to taste. (The dressing will keep for up to one month in a tightly closed jar in the refrigerator.)

Peel and core the apples and slice them into thin wedges, about 12 to an apple. Place them in a large bowl with all the remaining salad ingredients and mix well. Drizzle some of the dressing over and toss, then serve, with extra dressing on the side for those who want more.

SQUAB, PLUMS AND COBNUTS

SERVES

4 plums
1 tbsp sugar
glug of brandy
12 black peppercorns
2–3 sprigs of fresh thyme,
  leaves picked from stems
4 squabs
7 tbsp olive oil, plus extra
  for rubbing
1 tbsp vegetable oil
12 fresh, young cobnuts
  (hazelnuts)
2 handfuls of mixed salad
  leaves and sprouts
juice of 1 lemon
salt and pepper

This little salad is quick and very delicious. Cobnuts are another name for hazelnuts — "cob" is an old English word for head and a hazelnut is shaped like a bald head — and usually refers to the young, soft nuts before the shell has hardened.

Stew the plums in a little water with the sugar and brandy for 20 minutes, then let cool. Drain and slice thinly.

Meanwhile, preheat the oven to 350°F (175°C). Grind the whole peppercorns until fine and mix with 1 teaspoon of salt and the thyme leaves. Rub the squabs lightly with olive oil, then rub the pepper mixture all over the outside and inside of the birds.

Heat a large ovenproof frying pan until very hot. Add the vegetable oil and sear the squabs on all sides. Transfer the pan to the oven. At the same time, spread the nuts on a small baking sheet and put them in the oven to toast. Both the nuts and squabs will need 6–7 minutes.

Take everything from the oven and let cool. Cut the breasts from the squabs and slice thickly.

Put the toasted nuts, plums and salad leaves in a mixing bowl and pour the olive oil and lemon juice over. Add a generous grind of black pepper and a liberal sprinkle of salt. Mix well. Pile on plates, top with the sliced squab breasts, and serve.

SQUAB SALAD WITH PANCETTA AND BEANS

SERVES

8 oz (225 g) green beans, ends
   trimmed
4 oz (125 g) pancetta or bacon,
   cut into small strips
4 squabs
1 cup canned flageolet beans,
   rinsed and drained
3 heads Belgian endive,
   quartered lengthwise

DRESSING
7 tbsp extra-virgin olive oil
2 tbsp shallot vinegar
2 tsp strongly flavored *jus* or
   stock
2 tbsp diced shallots
salt and pepper

Bring a saucepan of salted water to a boil. Drop in the green beans. When the water returns to a boil, cook for 1 minute. Drain and refresh under cold running water. Set aside.

Preheat the oven to 400°F (200°C). Whisk all the ingredients for the dressing in a bain-marie or double boiler over steaming water until the mixture has emulsified. Set aside to cool.

In an ovenproof frying pan, fry the pancetta until golden. Use a slotted spoon to remove it from the pan and drain on paper towels. Season the squabs, then fry them in the fat left in the pan to give them some color. Transfer the pan to the oven and roast for 3–4 minutes.

When the squabs are done, drain off and reserve the pan juices. Strip the meat from the bones and cut the breast into thin strips.

In a large bowl, toss together the green beans, flageolets, pancetta and a little of the dressing, adding some of the pan juices from the squabs. Season well, then add the squab meat and toss again.

Arrange three pieces of endive on each serving plate and pile the salad on them. Finish with a little more of the dressing and some freshly ground pepper.

PARTRIDGE SALAD WITH ROAST PARSNIPS AND CHESTNUTS

SERVES

2 small parsnips, peeled and
   sliced into disks
olive oil
2 partridges
large handful of fresh thyme
   sprigs
1 large shallot, diced
4 large handfuls of arugula
   and Belgian endive or
   dandelion leaves
1 cup chopped roasted
   chestnuts
large handful of chopped
   fresh parsley
John's vinaigrette (page 101)
salt and pepper

Drink a big, heavy red wine with this rich autumn salad, to celebrate the transition to winter's gutsy foods after a summer of lettuce. It's best served at room temperature: Hot food and salad leaves do not mix well. They just turn to silage.

Preheat the oven to 325°F (160°C). Plunge the parsnip slices into a pan of boiling water and blanch for 2 minutes, then drain and pat dry. Drizzle with some olive oil and set aside.

Rub the partridges with oil, season well with salt and pepper and fill the cavities with the thyme. Set a ovenproof frying pan over medium heat. Once hot, add 1 tablespoon oil and the partridges. Cook, turning, until they are well colored all over.

Add the parsnips to the frying pan and transfer it to the oven. After 12 minutes give the pan a little shuffle, then cook for a few more minutes, at which point the partridges should be done.

Remove the partridges to a plate. Set the frying pan over medium heat, add the diced shallot and let the pan juices boil dry so all the flavor goes into the vegetables. Set aside to cool.

Toss the salad leaves together. Add the parsnips, chestnuts and parsley. Thinly slice the breast meat of the birds (keep the legs to make a pie) and add to the salad. Drizzle some vinaigrette over and toss. Pile the salad on plates and serve with warm bread.

PHEASANT SALAD WITH BEETS AND WATERCRESS

SERVES

2 pheasants

2 tbsp olive oil, plus extra
for rubbing

10 oz (285 g) cooked, peeled
beets

2 heaped tbsp red-currant jelly

1¹/₂ tbsp red wine vinegar

4 tbsp Caesar dressing
(page 94)

2 handfuls of watercress, thick
stems discarded

1 lb (450 g) fresh, crumbly
goat cheese

flaky sea salt and pepper

Beets are one of the most underused vegetables in the patch. I love them. To be lazy (like I am) buy them already cooked and peeled from the supermarket. By the way, my father's favorite sandwich was sliced beets with peanut butter. Strange but true.

Preheat the oven to 400°F (200°C). Heat a heavy ovenproof frying pan. Rub the pheasant with oil and seasoning and place in the hot pan. Cook, turning, until well colored, then transfer to the oven and roast for 15 minutes. When done, let cool, then shred the breast meat for the salad.

Meanwhile, cut the beets in quarters and place in a pan with the red-currant jelly and vinegar. Bring to a boil and cook, stirring, until the beets are well coated with sticky sauce, about 10 minutes. Set aside to cool.

When the beets are cold, mix them with the Caesar dressing and divide among six serving plates. Cover with a layer of watercress. If the goat cheese has any rind, remove it, then crumble the cheese into pieces and scatter over the watercress. Add the pheasant meat. Sprinkle the salads with salt, pepper and olive oil before serving.

CHICKEN LIVER SALAD

SERVES

12 chicken livers
1 tsp cracked black
   peppercorns
4 tbsp butter
1½ tbsp olive oil
splash of wine vinegar
4 tbsp Madeira or marsala
1 tbsp red-currant jelly
1 tsp Dijon mustard
2 handfuls of corn salad
   (mâche)
some other salad leaves, if
   desired
handful of fresh red currants
salt

A simple and quick salad, this is sweet from the fortified wine and sour from the currants.

Heat a frying pan. Season the livers with salt and cracked pepper. Add the butter and oil to the pan, then throw in the livers. Cook, tossing a few times, until they get a good color, about 5 minutes.

Add the vinegar and bring to a boil, letting it reduce by about half. Add the wine and boil again, then stir in the red-currant jelly and mustard and remove the pan from the heat.

Drain the sauce from the pan and mix a little of it with the leaves. Set up four plates and scatter the dressed leaves over them. Drop the red currants into the pan and toss. Divide the red currants and livers among the plates and drizzle the remaining sauce over.

You can make curry pastes easily in a food processor; however, using a pestle and mortar really is better as it will crush rather than rip the ingredients, resulting in a far better flavor. Using a pestle and mortar is also therapeutic, especially if you've got children.

You can of course use bought curry pastes instead, but be aware that the preservatives in them tend to give an acidic flavor. My recipes often include extra aromatics in the sauce to help counteract that.

The curry paste recipes in this chapter make more than you'll need for one dish, but it's not worth the trouble of preparing a smaller quantity. The excess will keep well in a glass jar in the refrigerator for two weeks. I like to divide mine into 2-tablespoon portions and store them in small plastic bags in the freezer, where they will keep for up to six months.

curries

THAI GREEN CHICKEN CURRY, MY WAY

SERVES

13/4 lb (800 g) skinless,
   boneless chicken thighs
2 cans (14 oz/400 g each)
   coconut milk
6 Kaffir lime leaves, shredded
3 lemongrass stalks, peeled
   and chopped
2 tbsp sliced galangal
1 tbsp palm sugar
1 tbsp fish sauce
handful of Thai pea eggplants
large handful of bean sprouts
large bunch of fresh Thai basil

GREEN CURRY PASTE
1/4 cup coriander seeds
1/4 cup cumin seeds
1 blade mace
1 tsp freshly grated nutmeg
9 garlic cloves, chopped
9 shallots, chopped
about 15 cilantro (coriander)
   stems with roots, chopped,
   plus leaves for garnish
19 fresh, long green chilies,
   deseeded and chopped
8 oz (225 g) galangal, chopped
5 lemongrass stalks, peeled
   and chopped
2 tsp salt
5 Kaffir lime leaves, chopped
31/2 oz (100 g) shrimp paste
handful of fresh Thai basil
   leaves

Don't let a green curry carry on cooking once the chicken is ready, otherwise the vibrant color will begin to turn gray. It will also start to taste bitter rather than fresh and spicy-hot.

To make the curry paste, heat a frying pan (without oil), add the dry spices, and toast until they begin to color and release their aromas. Remove from the heat and let them cool a bit, then grind to a powder in a spice mill or blender.

Using a blender or a mortar and pestle, blend or pound the garlic to break it down, then add the shallots and cilantro roots and continue processing. Work in the chilies, galangal, lemongrass and salt. Finally, add the lime leaves, shrimp paste, basil and ground spices, and blend or pound until you have a smooth paste.

Cut each chicken thigh into three; set aside. Do not shake the cans of coconut milk before opening them; just scrape the fatty top layer of the coconut milk into a warm (not smoking) wok. Cook it slowly, stirring all the time, until it starts to bubble and sizzle and just begins to split. Add about 3 tablespoons of the green curry paste (you may need a bit more if using a bought paste) and cook for a few moments until it releases its aroma.

Add the chicken, the rest of the coconut milk, the lime leaves, lemongrass, galangal, palm sugar and half the fish sauce. Let bubble until the oil in the coconut milk starts to come through to the surface, about 15 minutes.

Add the pea eggplants and the rest of the fish sauce and cook for a few minutes longer. Stir in the bean sprouts. Scatter the Thai basil and cilantro leaves on top and serve.

Tip: to make tamarind water, massage fresh tamarind paste in an equal volume of hot water until it is softened, then strain off the flavored liquid.

MASSAMAN CHICKEN AND SHRIMP CURRY

SERVES

½ cup coconut cream

1½ tbsp fish sauce

2 rounded tbsp palm sugar

4 tbsp tamarind water

2 cans (14 oz/400 g each)
  coconut milk

1 pineapple, peeled, cored and
  cut into large pieces

10 Kaffir lime leaves, torn

4 fresh, large red chilies, cut
  into pieces

2 lemongrass stalks, peeled
  and cut into 1½-inch
  (3.8 cm) pieces

6 skinless, boneless chicken
  thighs, each cut into 3 pieces

about 20 large raw shrimp,
  peeled and deveined

fresh Thai basil, for garnish

MASSAMAN CURRY PASTE

6 large, fresh red chilies,
  deseeded and chopped

2 lemongrass stalks, peeled
  and chopped

¼ cup chopped galangal

4 shallots, sliced

6 garlic cloves, chopped

1 Kaffir lime or regular lime,
  chopped

3 tbsp ground white pepper

2 oz (55 g) shrimp paste

⅔ oz (20 g) roasted dried
  shrimp

This is a complex but beautiful Thai curry, and although time consuming to make, it is worth the effort. Unlike many Thai dishes, you can serve it simply with some noodles or rice to give a whole meal. This recipe is for eight to 10 people, but even if there are just four of you I'll bet you finish it all.

To make the curry paste, put all the ingredients in a food processor and blend until smooth. Taste and add some salt, if necessary.

To make the curry, melt the coconut cream in a saucepan, stirring constantly to stop the cream burning. When it has separated, fry the curry paste in the fat until it is fragrant. Add the fish sauce, palm sugar and tamarind water. Cook until the mixture darkens.

Add the coconut milk and pineapple and bring to a boil. Throw in the lime leaves, chilies and lemongrass, then add the chicken. Return to a boil and cook for 3 minutes. Add the shrimp, bring back to a boil and cook for another 3 minutes.

Take the pan from the heat and leave it for 20 minutes to infuse while you cook your rice. Return the curry to the heat, bring it to a boil and cook for 3 minutes. Serve garnished with some Thai basil leaves.

CHICKEN DHANSAK

SERVES

LENTILS

1⅓ cups red lentils
vegetable oil
1 garlic clove, crushed
2 thumb-sized pieces of fresh
    ginger, peeled and smashed,
    then chopped
1 fresh, long red chili, chopped
1 large onion, chopped
1 tsp cardamom pods, crushed
2 large, ripe plum or Roma
    tomatoes, chopped
1¼ cups chicken stock
4 tbsp butter
handful of cilantro sprigs
salt

DRY CURRY

2 tbsp coriander seeds
3 small, dried red chilies
2 cloves
2 green cardamom pods
1 tsp cumin seeds
1 tsp ground fenugreek
1 tsp ground turmeric
1 tsp sea salt
7 tbsp ghee
3 large skinless, boneless
    chicken (or guinea fowl)
    breast halves, cubed
10 fresh or dried curry leaves

Here is an interesting curry, which is really more accurately described as a great big lentil casserole with loads of wonderful smoky flavors of fenugreek and curry leaves. You can use guinea fowl in place of chicken, if you like. This recipe easily serves up to eight people and will still give leftovers.

The day before cooking, put the lentils to soak in cold water overnight. Next day, drain the lentils, put them in a saucepan, cover with fresh water and add some salt. Bring to a boil and simmer until just tender. Remove from the heat and set aside.

Heat a little vegetable oil in a saucepan and fry the garlic, ginger, chili and onion gently until golden. Add the cardamom and cook for a few seconds, then add the tomatoes and stock. Add the contents of the lentil pan and cook for 10 minutes longer.

Take out half of the lentil mixture and puree it to a soup consistency. Stir this back into the remaining lentil mixture.

To make the dry chicken curry, toast all the spices, including the dried chilies and salt, in a heavy-based pan until they are colored and very fragrant. Let cool, then grind to a fine powder.

Melt the ghee in a wide, heavy-based pan and add the chicken (or guinea fowl) and curry leaves. Cook for a minute or so to give the meat a little color. Add the ground spices and turn the heat down low while you mix the chicken and spices well. Raise the heat and cook for 2–3 minutes.

Pour in the lentil mixture, stirring well, then cover and reduce the heat again. Cook for 8 minutes. Remove from the heat and let sit, covered, for 10 minutes. Stir in the butter, top with the cilantro and serve with flatbread for scooping.

DRY CEYLONESE CURRY WITH TURKEY

SERVES

14 oz (400 g) can coconut milk
about 6 shallots, finely sliced
3 garlic cloves, minced
thumb-sized piece of fresh
   ginger, peeled and minced
1–2 tsp hot chili powder
1/2 tsp ground turmeric
1 lemongrass stalk, peeled
   and smashed
2 inch (5 cm) piece screwpine
   (pandan) leaf (optional)
1 lb (450 g) turkey leg or
   thigh meat, cubed
juice of 1/2 lemon or lime
about 2 tbsp ghee

CEYLON CURRY POWDER
1/4 cup coriander seeds
1/4 cup cumin seeds
1 tsp fennel seeds
2-inch (5 cm) cinnamon stick
1/2 tsp cloves
1 tsp green cardamom pods
3/4 tsp ground fenugreek
10–12 curry leaves
1 tbsp raw rice

This is very similar to the Indonesian dish *rendang*, in which meat is boiled with coconut milk and spices. It is really more of a relish, with a marmalade-like sauce cloaking the meat. Serve with sticky rice or even little lettuce leaves for wrapping — it's a hot, sweet and sticky snack rather than a curry main dish.

Turkey leg or thigh is best, because breast meat would become too dry (pheasant and guinea fowl are other possibilities). Let it cook down really well: the meat will go through stages from tough to very tender and falling apart, which is where you want it to be.

To make the curry powder, toast the spices and curry leaves in a hot, dry pan until fragrant (do not let them burn or the curry will taste bitter). Remove from the pan, then toast the rice. Let cool, then grind the spices and rice to a fine powder using either a spice mill or a mortar and pestle.

Shake the can of coconut milk well, then open it and pour into a pot. Add half the shallots and garlic, then stir in the ginger, chili powder, turmeric, lemongrass, screwpine leaf and 3–4 tablespoons of the Ceylon curry powder.

Pour in 1 cup of water and bring to a boil, stirring well. Mix in the turkey and lemon or lime juice. Simmer over medium heat, stirring occasionally, until the meat is cooked and the curry is thick, about 20 minutes.

Shortly before serving, heat the ghee in a frying pan or wok and fry the remaining shallots and garlic until aromatic and golden brown. Add them to the curry and stir well.

MALAYSIAN POTATO AND DUCK CURRY

SERVES

1½ cups raw cashews or
   candlenuts

2 green onions, minced

vegetable oil

2 lemongrass stalks

6 tbsp ground coriander

1 tsp cumin seeds

1 tsp ground turmeric

3½ oz (100 g) block coconut
   cream

3 large shallots, minced

6 garlic cloves, chopped

6 fresh red chilies, deseeded
   and chopped

2 thumb-sized pieces of fresh
   ginger, peeled and chopped

2 bay leaves

2¼–2½ lb (1–1.1 kg) duck leg
   and thigh meat, cut into
   1½-inch (3.8 cm) cubes

2 cans (14 oz/400 g each)
   coconut milk

2 cups chicken, vegetable or
   other stock, heated

20 new potatoes, peeled

You can use duck breast here if you want to, but it tends to get a bit dry. Whatever pan you choose should be wide rather than deep because the liquid in the curry needs to boil away.

Bring a small pan of water to a boil and throw in the cashews or candlenuts. Remove from the heat and drain the nuts, then crush them to a paste in a mortar. Stir in the green onions. Heat a little oil in a small pan and fry the nut paste until it is fragrant and lightly colored. Set aside to use as a garnish.

Using a mortar and pestle, pound the lemongrass to a pulp, then remove from the mortar and set aside. In a frying pan, toast the coriander, cumin seeds and turmeric gently until fragrant, then grind to a fine powder in the mortar or using a spice mill.

In a wide pot or wok, heat the block of coconut cream until it melts, keeping the heat low so it does not burn. Drop in the shallots, garlic, chilies and ginger, and cook gently until the shallots have softened and the mixture smells beautifully fragrant. Add the toasted ground spices and the bay leaves. Fry for a few more minutes.

Add the duck and increase the heat. Brown it well for a few minutes, stirring to coat it completely in the spices. Add the coconut milk and bring to a boil, then add the hot stock. Turn the heat up to high and continue cooking for 20 minutes — the level of the liquid will quickly fall.

Add the potatoes. Reduce the temperature so that the sauce just bubbles and continue cooking very gently until the sauce is like lava and really coats the meat and spuds, about 1 hour. Don't let the mixture simmer any harder or the potatoes will break up. Finally, top the curry with the nut paste and serve.

MATT DAWSON'S CREAMY TURKEY KORMA

SERVES

2 tbsp vegetable oil

1 lb (450 g) turkey thigh meat, cubed

1 red onion, thinly sliced

1 red pepper, chopped

1 zucchini, sliced or chopped

2 garlic cloves, crushed

2 tbsp korma curry paste

1/2 tsp hot chili paste or powder

1 cup canned crushed tomatoes

2/3 cup chicken stock

2/3 cup heavy cream

1/4 cup chopped coconut cream

bunch of cilantro, chopped

salt and pepper

Matt Dawson is a British rugby player, and a very good cook who understands what people like to eat. This dish, which he created for a celebrity recipe challenge, is what he likes to eat, and it's delicious.

Heat the oil in a large pot and, working in batches, fry the cubed turkey until lightly browned, 2–3 minutes per batch. Remove the turkey, allowing the excess oil to drain back into the pan, and set it aside.

Add the onion to the hot pot and fry until soft, about 5 minutes. Add the red pepper, zucchini and garlic, and continue cooking for 5 minutes, stirring occasionally. Stir in the curry and chili pastes, then add the tomatoes and stock. Bring to a simmer. Return the turkey to the pot and cook gently for 10 minutes.

Stir in the cream and coconut. Cook until the coconut has melted and the sauce is bubbling, 1–2 minutes longer. Season to taste, and sprinkle with the cilantro before serving with naan or rice and some mango chutney.

TURKEY AND SAAG ALOO

SERVES

2 tbsp ground coriander

2 tbsp ground cumin

2 tbsp ground turmeric

2 tsp salt

1 tsp mustard seeds

1 tsp hot chili powder

4 garlic cloves, sliced

3 fresh, long red chilies, sliced
   (remove the seeds, if you
   prefer)

1/2 cup ghee or clarified butter

2 large onions, diced

1 large potato, peeled and cut
   into cubes

1 lb (450 g) skinless turkey
   breast meat, cut into
   thumb-sized chunks

7 oz (200 g) large leaf spinach

2 tbsp plain yogurt

small bunch of cilantro

I have always loved spinach and potatoes cooked with huge amounts of spice. Here I've added turkey, which is meant to be a good lean meat, but I have fixed that with the addition of lots of butter. This is what food should taste like! You don't need a lot, though, so have more rice than curry. Enjoy.

Toast the dry spices and salt in a hot pan until they start to smell smoky, just a minute or so. Transfer to a mortar with the garlic and two of the chillies and crush to a paste.

Heat the ghee or clarified butter in a heavy-based pan. Add the onions and fry until golden. Add the spice mix, then turn the heat down. Add the potatoes and mix well. Keep frying for a few minutes, then pour in 1/2 cup water. Turn the heat up and bring to a boil. Cover and cook for 10 minutes, checking that the water does not evaporate completely.

Add the turkey and stir well, scraping the bottom of the pan to pick up any good bits. If the curry is dry, add a little more water. Cook for 5 minutes. Add the spinach and a little more water if the mixture seems to need it. Cook for 5 minutes longer, stirring constantly, then cover the pan, remove it from the heat and leave the spinach to steam for 2 minutes.

Take about 2 tablespoons of the spinach, combine it with half the yogurt, and puree this mixture in a blender. Stir the puree back into the curry and let it heat through for a moment. Transfer to a warmed serving dish and top with the rest of the yogurt, the remaining sliced red chili and the cilantro.

JUNGLE CURRY OF GUINEA FOWL

SERVES

2/3 cup vegetable oil

3 1/2 tbsp fish sauce

1 guinea fowl, cut up into
  8 pieces

1/2 cup Shaoxing wine

2 quarts (8 cups) chicken stock
  or water

7 oz (200 g) snake beans
  (Chinese long beans) or
  green beans, cut into 3-inch
  (7.5 cm) pieces

handful of snow peas

7 oz (200 g) bamboo shoots,
  cut into pieces

bunch of fresh Thai basil,
  leaves picked from stems

3 1/2 oz (100 g) karachi stalks
  or fresh ginger, scraped and
  cut into strips

30 Kaffir lime leaves, torn

7 oz (200 g) bok choy or choy
  sum, trimmed and divided
  into stems

small bunch of fresh mint

YELLOW CURRY PASTE

1 oz (30 g) dried shrimp

1/3 oz (10 g) shrimp paste

3 garlic cloves, chopped

6 red shallots, chopped

2 oz (55 g) galangal, chopped

19 fresh, long yellow chilies,
  deseeded and chopped

2 tsp salt

2/3 oz (20 g) fresh turmeric

The jungle curry has its roots in the north of Thailand near the border with China. Coconuts do not grow in the north and so the area's traditional curries tend to contain more water and flavorings such as rich Chinese Shaoxing wine. This sauce tastes deep and strong, so holds up well against rich meats like guinea fowl or even pheasant and partridge.

First, make the curry paste. Soak the dried shrimp in water for about 30 minutes, then drain. Meanwhile, wrap the shrimp paste in foil and toast it in a hot, dry pan until fragrant. Process the garlic and shallots in a blender (or pound in a mortar). Add the galangal, chilies and salt, followed by the shrimp paste, drained dried shrimp and turmeric. Blend to a paste.

To make the curry, heat the oil in a wok or large saucepan and stir-fry 2 tablespoons of the curry paste until it becomes fragrant, 2–3 minutes. Add the fish sauce and continue frying for 1 minute. Add the guinea fowl pieces to the wok and cook with the paste for 5 minutes, so they get a little color. Pour in the wine and then the chicken stock or water. Bring to a simmer and let cook for 40 minutes.

Add the remaining ingredients and simmer for 1 more minute, then remove from the heat. Cover and let the curry rest for 5 minutes so the flavors can infuse before serving.

PARTRIDGE IN CHILI JAM

SERVES

3 partridges
½ cup lard or vegetable oil,
  plus extra oil for frying
  the birds
1 heaped cup palm sugar
5 tsp fish sauce
7 oz (200 g) gai lan (Chinese
  broccoli)
about 5 Kaffir lime leaves,
  chopped
large handful of fresh Thai
  basil, chopped
deep-fried garlic and chili
  slices, for garnish

CURRY PASTE
⅓ oz (10 g) dried red chilies
1 oz (30 g) dried red shrimp
9 large, fresh red chilies (e.g.
  serranos), deseeded and
  chopped
1 red onion, chopped
17 garlic cloves
2½ oz (70 g) galangal, peeled
  and chopped
⅓ oz (10 g) cilantro (coriander)
  roots, chopped
3 lemongrass stalks, peeled
  and chopped

First make the curry paste. Snap the stalk ends from the dried chilies and shake out and discard the seeds. Place the chilies in a bowl, cover with hot water and let soak for about 30 minutes to plump up. Meanwhile, soak the dried shrimp in a bowl of cold water for 30 minutes or so.

Set up a steamer big enough to hold the birds. Cook them over gently simmering water for 30 minutes. Remove from the heat, but leave the birds in the steamer.

Drain the soaked chillies and shrimp. Put them in a blender with all the other ingredients for the curry paste and blend to a coarse paste. Alternatively, pound them with a mortar and pestle. You may need to add a little water to bring the paste together, but try to add as little as possible, because the ingredients (particularly the soaked chilies and shrimp) contain their own moisture.

Heat the lard or vegetable oil in a heavy-based pan and add the curry paste. You need to cook it very slowly, taking care that it doesn't stick to the bottom of the pan and burn, until all the moisture has disappeared, about 2 hours — yes, 2 hours! After an hour or so, add the palm sugar and 3 teaspoons of the fish sauce. When the chili jam is ready, it will have become very aromatic and the color will have deepened to a rich red-brown. At this point you can take it off the heat and keep it on one side until you are ready to fry the partridges.

Strip the meat from the birds and cut it into finger-sized pieces. Heat a wok with a little vegetable oil, add the partridge meat, and fry until it starts to get a little color and the skin becomes crisp. Stir in the gai lan. Add a couple of spoonfuls of chili jam and toss well. Add a few drops of fish sauce and continue cooking until thoroughly hot — it should be sticky, hot and sweet. Scatter the lime leaves, Thai basil and some deep-fried garlic and chili slices over the top and serve.

Tip: the best Thai fish sauce is the Squid brand, which you can buy for the equivalent of a few cents in Thailand. It is exported relatively cheaply in big bottles that will keep for quite a long time (the sauce will darken and mature gently).

A barbecue is not just for summer. Nor is it only about boys and beer — and burned food. Grilling over coals is a wonderful way to cook, but one that needs a bit of practice and patience. What we Australians call a barbie can be a little special, too, so why not welcome your friends with a glass of champagne?

You can grill all year round. It may feel a little strange the first time you stand outside wearing a hat and gloves while cooking, but there is real romance in eating summery-flavored grilled chicken or duck as the snow falls outside.

When cooking over coals, remember: if there are flames, it ain't ready. Grilling a piece of chicken, duck or turkey is not quick, if you want it to be beautifully smoky and crisp outside and succulent and tender inside. The trick is to find the hot spots and cool spots of the grill. Some things you want to sear over high heat, while others you want to put over high heat to start off, to get some color, and then move to a slightly cooler area to cook through. For more on grilling chicken breast and leg pieces, see page 62.

barbecue

GRILLING KEBABS

The idea of making up some little skewers, or even big skewers, and cooking them quickly over hot coals is a good one. Various things can be used to spear your ingredients: rosemary twigs, bamboo sticks, big metal skewers — you can even cook little marinated hunks on wooden toothpicks and serve them as a canapé.

Whatever you choose, always soak any wood or herb branch in water for at least 10 minutes before threading the meat on it for grilling. This will stop it bursting into flames.

Aim to marinate raw poultry for at least 2–3 hours, to let the flavors soak in, and remember to keep a bit of the marinade back to brush over the food while it is on the grill.

When you're ready to cook, the coals should be glowing, but there shouldn't be any flame. If you are using a grill pan indoors, keep the heat around medium. If it is all too hot, your chunks of meat will be burned on the outside but not cooked through.

All the recipes that follow use thigh or breast meat. In general I prefer the former. Keep the skin on when using lean breast meat — it needs protecting from the intense and direct heat if it is to stay moist. You can always remove the skin when serving.

It's common to cut poultry into cubes for kebabs, but there are exceptions, such as for satay, when the meat is traditionally cut in strips. For satay you need to thread the meat strips on the skewers so that the maximum amount is exposed — that way, when the skewers are put on the hot grill they cook quickly and the meat stays moist.

OREGANO AND GARLIC

10 garlic cloves
1 tsp salt
1 tsp freshly ground black pepper
1/2 cup olive oil
handful of fresh oregano, minced
6 boneless chicken thighs or breast halves

Crush the garlic to a paste and season well with salt
and pepper. Mix in the olive oil followed by the
oregano. Cut the chicken into 3/4-inch (2 cm) cubes.
Add to the flavored oil and mix well. Let marinate for
20 minutes.

Thread about six cubes of chicken onto each of
12 skewers (rosemary stalks would be good for this).
Place the kebabs on the grill and cook for about
12 minutes, turning them every 3 minutes so that
the meat is well colored all over. Great with spiced
couscous and a big salad. MAKES 12.

CHICKEN TIKKA

6 boneless chicken breast halves, each cut into 4 strips
juice of 1 lemon
large pinch of salt
1 tsp ground turmeric
2 dried red chilies, or 1 tsp hot chili powder
1 tsp cumin seeds
1/2 tsp coriander seeds
pinch of asafetida
a little white pepper
1 cup plain yogurt

Put the chicken in a bowl and sprinkle with the lemon
juice and salt. To make the paste, toast the spices in a
hot, dry pan until fragrant and about to smoke. Crush
to a powder, then combine with the yogurt. Drain the
lemon juice from the chicken, then pour the spiced
yogurt over the chicken and rub it in well.

Thread two strips of chicken onto each skewer so
that they are long rather than bunched up. Grill for
3 minutes, then turn and brush the cooked portion
with some of the leftover yogurt marinade. Continue
cooking, turning and basting for about 12 minutes in
total. Serve the tikkas with flatbread. MAKES 12.

CHICKEN AND SHRIMP WITH PANCETTA

1 garlic clove, chopped
1/2 cup olive oil
pared zest and juice of 1 lemon
24 large raw shrimp, peeled and deveined
6 skinless, boneless chicken breast halves,
   each cut into 8
24 slices pancetta or bacon
48 fresh basil leaves
salt and pepper
lemon wedges and mayonnaise, for serving

Mix the garlic, oil, lemon zest and juice, and some salt
and pepper in a bowl. Add the shrimp and let marinate
for at least 10 minutes, then add the chicken.

Lay a piece of pancetta on a work surface and place
a basil leaf on top. Lay a shrimp on this, then add
another basil leaf. Wrap the pancetta around the
shrimp. Repeat to wrap all the shrimp.

Thread the wrapped shrimp and pieces of chicken
onto skewers, alternating them so that you have four
pieces of chicken and two shrimp on each skewer.

Grill, turning regularly, for about 10 minutes. Serve
with lemon and mayo. MAKES 12.

SATAY

1/2 cup light soy sauce
1 cup mirin
6 tbsp miso paste
1 lb (450 g) skinless, boneless chicken breast,
   cut into 1/4-inch (0.6 cm) strips
PEANUT SAUCE
1 shallot, diced
4 tbsp vegetable oil
1 tbsp Thai red curry paste
2 small, fresh red chilies, deseeded and minced
1 1/4 cups freshly ground peanuts or crunchy
   peanut butter
4 tbsp soy sauce
large handful of chopped cilantro

For the sauce, soften the shallot in the oil for 3 minutes.
Add the curry paste and chilies. Cook, stirring, until
fragrant, about 5 minutes. Mix in the peanuts and 1 cup
water. Bring to a boil. Add the soy sauce and set aside.

Mix together the soy sauce, mirin and miso, then stir
in the chicken. Let marinate for 20 minutes. Thread
onto skewers. Grill, turning every 30 seconds or so, for
3–4 minutes. Stir the cilantro into the sauce and serve
with the satay. SERVES 4–6.

PAPRIKA CHICKEN WITH FENNEL, TOMATO AND PARSLEY SALAD

3 plum or Roma tomatoes
1 fennel bulb, thinly shaved
2/3 cup black olives, pitted
juice of 1 lemon
olive oil
6 boneless chicken breast halves, cut into 1 1/2–2-inch
   (3.8–5 cm) chunks
2 garlic cloves, crushed
2 tsp hot smoked paprika
large handful of fresh flat-leaf parsley, roughly chopped
salt and pepper

Chop the tomatoes roughly, squeezing out as much juice as possible. Put them in a large mixing bowl with the fennel, olives, lemon juice, 4 teaspoons olive oil and a large pinch of salt. Mix with vigor. Set aside.

Mix the chicken with 4 tablespoons olive oil, the garlic, paprika and some salt and pepper. Thread the meat onto skewers. Grill for 15 minutes, turning every couple of minutes to lightly char each side. Stir the parsley through the salad and serve with the kebabs, plus some grilled vegetables on the side. SERVES 6

CHINESE CHICKEN WITH SESAME SEEDS

This is a simple marinade that can be used for chunks or even whole breasts of chicken.

4 tbsp honey
4 tbsp soy sauce
4 tbsp dry sherry
2 green onions, thinly sliced
1 1/2 tbsp ketchup
4 tbsp oyster sauce
1/3 cup sesame seeds
6 skinless, boneless chicken breast halves,
   each cut into 3 strips

In a saucepan, heat the honey with the soy sauce and sherry. When it is starting to boil, remove from the heat. Add the green onions and let cool a little. Add the ketchup and oyster sauce and stir well, then add the sesame seeds. Marinate the chicken in this mixture for at least 10 minutes before threading the strips onto skewers and grilling.

Return the remaining marinade to the saucepan and bring to a boil. When the chicken is cooked, spoon the marinade over the kebabs. Serve with lettuce cups and some more green onions. SERVES 6.

GREEN CURRY

6 boneless chicken breast halves
14 oz (400 g) can coconut milk
2 tbsp green curry paste, bought or homemade
   (page 112)
handful of chopped cilantro

Cut the chicken into even-sized pieces. Mix the coconut milk with the green curry paste and the chopped cilantro. Add the chicken and let marinate for a few hours or overnight.

Thread the chicken onto skewers. Lay them skin-side down over glowing coals and grill for 3–4 minutes. Turn them over and cook for 3–4 minutes on the other side. Turn again and cook for 3 minutes longer. SERVES 6.

SPICED YOGURT

10 boneless chicken thighs
juice of 2 lemons
3 sprigs of fresh thyme, leaves picked from stems
1 cup plain yogurt
2 fresh red chilies, deseeded
2 garlic cloves
2 tbsp chopped cilantro
large pinch of ground cinnamon
large pinch of ground cardamom
large pinch of ground cloves
large pinch of ground turmeric
salt and pepper

Rub the chicken with a mixture of the lemon juice, 1 tablespoon of salt and the thyme leaves. Leave for a few hours. When ready to proceed, put the yogurt, chilies, garlic, cilantro and ground spices in a food processor and blend to make a paste. Rub this all over the chicken and let marinate (preferably overnight).

Thread onto skewers and grill, turning regularly, for about 20 minutes. Serve with skordalia (page 80), flatbread and tzatziki. SERVES 6.

BUTTERFLIED POUSSIN WITH GARLIC

SERVES 🐔🐔🐔🐔🐔🐔🐔🐔🐔🐔

3 tbsp salt
1 tbsp ground black pepper
½ cup olive oil
10 butterflied poussins
   or squab chickens, or
   3 butterflied chickens
40 garlic cloves (yes 40!)
handful of fresh rosemary
   sprigs

I believe that poultry needs a little fat for flavor and crisp skin for both flavor and texture, but I also understand that not everyone likes the fat. This dish satisfies both ways of thinking: the fat melts away while the meat is cooking and the skin goes crisp.

Mix together the salt, pepper and olive oil. Poke the skin side of the birds with a sharp knife to make slits just big enough to fit a clove of garlic — about four slits in each poussin, or more if you're using chicken. Don't fill the slits with garlic yet; you'll do that later. Rub the seasoned olive oil over the birds, then cover well and refrigerate for 1 hour, or preferably overnight.

When ready to proceed, peel the garlic and cut the rosemary into pieces ¾ inch (2 cm) long. Put one whole garlic clove and a bit of rosemary in each slit you made in the poultry.

When the coals are ready, place the butterflied birds skin-side down on the grill and cook until well colored, about 10 minutes. Turn the birds over and grill until well colored on the other side, about 10 minutes. Then cover the barbecue and continue cooking for 10 minutes or so on each side. Serve with a salad of avocado, baby spinach and toasted pine nuts.

GROUND CHICKEN ON LEMONGRASS

MAKES

12 lemongrass stalks
4 cilantro (coriander) roots, chopped
7 white peppercorns, crushed
2 Thai shallots, very finely sliced
2 tsp fish sauce
1 extra-large egg white
1 Kaffir lime leaf, finely shredded
1½ cups ground chicken

This is one of those recipes that Thais disagree about. Some say the "real" recipe calls for the chicken to be wrapped around sugarcane rather than lemongrass, so the sugarcane gives a caramel sweetness to the chicken. Either way, it tastes great.

Trim the lemongrass at both ends to create a stick about the same length as a pencil. Peel away about four layers, then bruise the stalks well to release their flavor. Let soak in cold water for about 10 minutes. Meanwhile, pound the cilantro roots and peppercorns together in a mortar to form a paste.

Mix all the ingredients except the lemongrass together in a large bowl. Divide the mixture into 12 pieces and shape one around the end of each stalk of lemongrass. Grill gently for about 15 minutes, turning frequently and occasionally splashing the chicken with water to keep it moist.

SPICED CHICKEN PATTY WITH TOMATO SALSA

SERVES

thumb-sized piece of fresh
  ginger, peeled
1 garlic clove
4 white peppercorns, or some
  ground white pepper
handful of cilantro sprigs
1 tsp vegetable oil
1 lb (450 g) ground chicken
2 handfuls of fresh white
  bread crumbs
2 eggs, beaten

SALSA
2 tbsp vegetable oil
2 tsp ground cumin
1 tsp ground coriander
1 tsp ground turmeric
1 onion, finely chopped
1 garlic clove, crushed
1¼ cups tomato puree or
  canned crushed tomatoes
salt and pepper

These little beauties are full of ginger and spice, but should not be too overpowering, because you still want to taste the chicken. The recipe works just as well with turkey. I love the spicy salsa.

Pound the ginger, garlic, white pepper and cilantro together to make a paste, then add the oil. Mix the chicken, bread crumbs, eggs, spice paste and some salt together with your hands in a large bowl until well combined.

Shape into six balls and flatten them into patties. Chill for 2 hours before cooking so that the mixture has a chance to set.

To make the salsa, heat the oil in a frying pan. Add the spices and cook for 1 minute, then add the onion and stir for a few minutes until the onion is translucent. Add the garlic and cook for 1 more minute. Pour in the tomato puree or crushed tomatoes and bring to a boil. Cook for 10 minutes. Season well with salt and pepper.

Grill the patties for 10 minutes, turning them over halfway through cooking. Serve with the salsa, in buns with some arugula if desired.

CHICKEN BURGERS

SERVES

1 medium onion, roughly
   chopped
large handful of fresh flat-leaf
   parsley
2 tbsp ketchup
1 tbsp oyster sauce
$1^{1}/_{4}$ lb (560 g) fresh bulk pork
   sausage
$1^{1}/_{4}$ lb (560 g) ground chicken
1 egg plus 1 egg yolk

FOR SERVING
8 slices bacon
8 eggs (optional)
8 burger buns
8 slices good melting cheese
butter
tomato relish

Chicken burgers need to be big and juicy. I add bulk sausage, with a good amount of fat through it, and beat in a little water to keep the burgers really moist. My other little secret is to use Chinese oyster sauce instead of salt to season the mixture.

Put the onion, parsley, ketchup and oyster sauce in a food processor and blend to a paste. Combine the sausage and ground chicken in a mixing bowl and add the onion mixture, whole egg and egg yolk, and 4 tablespoons water. Beat — and I mean really beat — together. Divide the mix into eight and roll into large balls, then flatten slightly. Refrigerate for at least an hour.

When the coals are ready, place the burgers on the grill and leave for a few minutes until the edges start to color. Turn them over and cook for a few more minutes. Turn them again and move them to the side or a place where the heat is less intense. Continue cooking for 15 minutes; they will be well done.

While the burgers are cooking, fry the bacon (and eggs if you fancy them — I love burgers and eggs). Cut the buns open and toast them lightly on the cut sides.

Stack the burgers and bacon on the bases of the buns. Top each one with a slice of cheese, which should start to soften and melt. Spread the toasted side of the bun tops with butter and add some tomato relish. Set a fried egg (if using) on top of the cheese and cover with the bun tops. Stick a wooden skewer through the middle to hold it all together. Don't forget the napkins.

JERK CHICKEN

SERVES

12 chicken thighs (or 8 large
   chicken breast halves)

MARINADE
large bunch of green onions
2 tbsp soy sauce
2 tbsp vegetable oil
1 tbsp salt
juice of 1 lime
$\frac{1}{2}$ tsp dried thyme, or 1 tbsp
   fresh thyme leaves
1 tbsp allspice berries
1–10 Scotch bonnet chilies
   (start with a small amount
   and add more later if you
   want this hotter)
thumb-sized piece of fresh
   ginger
3 garlic cloves
$\frac{1}{2}$ small onion
2–3 tbsp brown sugar

To get a more authentic jerk flavor, add some wood chips to your barbecue and cook the chicken thighs over slow, indirect heat. Alternatively, enjoy a beautiful jerk chicken breast cooked over high heat — it should be ready in 10 minutes or less.

To make the marinade, put all the ingredients in a blender and blend until you have a puree. Don't add more water if you're having trouble getting it all blended; just keep turning off the blender, stirring it up with a spatula and trying again. Eventually it will start to blend up nicely. Now taste it. It should be pretty salty, but not unpleasantly puckeringly salty. You can also now throw in more chilies if it's not spicy enough for you. If you think it tastes too salty and sour, try adding a bit more brown sugar until things seem good and balanced.

Put the chicken pieces in a bowl, cover with the marinade and leave overnight. Next day, grill the chicken thighs over a smoky fire for 15–20 minutes, turning about six times during cooking.

RICE AND PEAS

SERVES

1¹/₃ cups long-grain rice
²/₃ cup basmati rice
¹/₂ cup coconut cream
2 large white onions, finely
  chopped
1 ham or bacon bone with a bit
  of meat left on it
2 bushy sprigs of fresh thyme
1 Scotch bonnet chili, left
  whole
1¹/₂ oz (40 g) saltfish, soaked in
  water overnight (optional)
14 oz (400 g) can coconut milk
14 oz (400 g) can red kidney
  beans or black-eyed peas,
  drained
2 cups chicken stock or
  ham stock
salt and pepper

If you want to add the saltfish to this traditional Jamaican dish, look for it in Caribbean markets.

Mix the two rices together. Rinse them thoroughly and drain. In a heavy pot, melt the coconut cream, then add the onions and fry gently until translucent. Add the ham bone, thyme, chili and saltfish (if using). Add the rice and coconut milk and bring slowly to a simmer.

Add the beans and half the stock and bring back to a simmer. Turn the heat down to its lowest setting. Season with salt and pepper, then cover and let cook gently for 20–30 minutes, stirring occasionally and adding more stock as necessary.

When the rice is cooked, remove from the heat and let stand with the lid on for 10 minutes. Discard the ham bone, thyme and chili before serving.

HOT WINGS
AND DRUMSTICKS

SERVES

1 cup ketchup
1/2 cup light soy sauce
1/2 cup olive oil
4 tbsp Worcestershire sauce
1 1/2 tbsp Tabasco sauce
  (optional)
1 garlic clove, crushed
1 egg yolk
12 chicken wings
12 chicken drumsticks

Chicken wings are very tasty. They have a lot of skin, but that skin cooks to become crisp and delicious, especially when the wings have been left in a quality marinade for a good period. The joy of sucking the meat from the wings fresh from the barbie is great. Kids love them — they are allowed to eat with their fingers after all.

The night before, mix together the ketchup, soy sauce, olive oil, Worcestershire sauce, Tabasco (if using) and garlic. Stir well, then mix in the egg yolk. Clean the wings and drumsticks of any feathers or yucky bits, then drop them into the marinade and leave overnight. If short on time, try to marinate them for a few hours at least.

Get your fire ready. Once the coals are white with a little ash, place the wings and drumsticks on the grill. Leave for a few minutes, then start to move them around. If the coals start to flare, take the chicken pieces off briefly or move them more often — this is just a result of the fat being broken down. I cook wings and drumsticks for about 20 minutes so the outside is well colored and the skin is starting to crisp.

When cooked, pile up on a large plate and serve, with plenty of napkins and maybe a couple of finger bowls.

GREEK-STYLE CHICKEN WITH FETA, TOMATOES AND OLIVES

SERVES

12 boneless chicken thighs
10 garlic cloves, crushed
1 tsp flaky sea salt
handful of rosemary leaves
juice of 2 lemons
1 cup olive oil
large handful of fresh flat-leaf
  parsley
large handful of fresh oregano
  or marjoram
1/2 cup diced plum or Roma
  tomatoes
1 1/3 cups pitted black olives
7 oz (200 g) feta cheese

The Greeks are clever cooks who use lesser cuts of high-quality meat for flavor, but also marinate them to tenderize the flesh. This recipe is a prime example.

Use a sharp knife to score the skin of the chicken, then lay the thighs out flat in a large dish. Mix together the garlic, salt, rosemary, lemon juice and half of the olive oil. Pour this over the chicken, rubbing it in well. Let marinate for an hour or so.

In a food processor, blend the parsley and oregano or marjoram with the remaining olive oil. Pour half of this mixture over the chicken and give it a good stir.

Mix the tomatoes with the olives and remaining herb oil. Set aside.

Grill the marinated chicken thighs, giving them a good blast of heat for 2 minutes before turning them over. Lift them a little higher or away from the coals, or move to a cooler part of the grill, and cook for 15 minutes or so, turning often.

When the chicken is cooked, place it on a large, flat serving dish. Sprinkle with the tomato, olive and herb mixture, then crumble the feta cheese over and serve.

STUFFED CHICKEN WITH OLIVES AND ARTICHOKES

SERVES

1 large leek

1 tbsp butter

olive oil, for drizzling

6 large chicken breast halves

$^2/_3$ cup mixed olives, pitted

1 cup artichoke hearts packed in olive oil, drained

1 fresh red chili, deseeded and minced

7 oz (200 g) ricotta or feta cheese

1 egg

1 lemon, halved or quartered

salt and pepper

Serve a good salad as a first course and then this terrific chicken with some extra artichokes and olives.

Clean the leek, splitting it down the center to make long, flat strips. Bring a pot of water to a boil with the butter and some salt and pepper. Plunge the leek into the boiling water and cook for 3 minutes, then drain and cool under running cold water. Put the leek in a bowl, pour over some olive oil, season and set aside.

Lay a chicken breast skin-side up on the work surface, with the pointed end of the breast closest to you. Take a sharp knife and make a slit in the chicken from the top right all the way down the side, so that the breast can be opened out to resemble a butterfly. Keeping the knife parallel to the board should make this a little easier. Repeat the process until all the breasts are done, and lay them out ready to be filled.

Squash the olives roughly. Chop the artichokes but not too finely. Mix the olives and artichokes with the chili and ricotta or feta to make the filling. In a separate small bowl, beat the egg and set aside.

Take a heaped spoonful of the filling and place on the center of each open chicken breast. Brush the edges of each breast with beaten egg, then fold the chicken up around the filling to make a parcel, tucking in all the edges.

Lay two pieces of leek flat and place a filled chicken breast on top. Wrap the leek around it and secure the ends of the leeks to the breast with a few wooden toothpicks. Repeat until all the filled chicken breasts are wrapped.

Place the parcels on the grill and cook for 5 minutes on each side, then repeat so they cook for about 20 minutes in total. Before serving, squeeze some lemon juice over them, sprinkle with ground black pepper and drizzle some olive oil over.

BARBECUED DUCK

SERVES

1 jar hoisin sauce
1 duck, all bones removed (you
   may need to have your
   butcher do this)
green onions, for garnish

Because duck has a good amount of fat in it that needs to be melted and the meat needs to be cooked slowly or it will be tough, it can only really be finished off on the grill. This dish is inspired by Chinese roast duck, or Peking duck, and it is fabulous.

Take a very big, deep pot and fill it three-fourths full with cold water. Stir in the hoisin sauce, then put in the duck. Set the pot over medium heat and slowly bring the water to a boil — this should take 20–30 minutes. As soon as the water is boiling, turn the heat down and cook gently for 15 minutes. Then turn off the heat and let the duck cool in the liquid for 3 hours.

Lift the duck out and pat it dry with paper towels.

Get your fire ready. Lay the duck skin-side down on the grill and cook until the skin starts to color. Turn the duck over and cook for 5 more minutes. Continue turning and cooking until the duck is cooked well on both sides — the skin should be crisp and well colored and the meat soft.

Take the duck from the grill, carve and serve garnished with green onions. Alternatively, slice it very thinly and serve in a flour tortilla with some diced tomatoes, shredded green onions and cilantro leaves.

As I have already said, if you can roast a chicken you can survive. Roasting is one of the seven principles of cooking, and, once mastered, such a useful skill. I have given guides on the temperatures and timings that work for me, but all ovens are different so you will need to feel your way a little.

The first rule of roasting is that whatever you roast needs to have some oil or fat to conduct the heat and keep the bird moist. The second and only other rule is all about the oven: Once at temperature and once the bird and all its accompanying bits are in it, *shut the door and keep it closed*. Every time you open the oven door the cold air goes in and the temperature inside drops and slows down the cooking process. More importantly, when you are roasting a whole bird you rely on the bones to conduct the heat; the cold air rushing in cools the bones so the heat doesn't get in deep. The result of this will be a dry, overcooked exterior and breast and undercooked legs and thighs. So try to open the oven door only when really necessary — when something needs to be added to your roast, or if it's on fire!

roasts

CHICKEN WITH OLIVES
AND LEMONS

SERVES

1 large chicken
3 whole lemons, quartered
24 big green and purple olives
2¼ lb (1 kg) new potatoes
4 tbsp olive oil
salt and pepper

This is a very easy but satisfying, full-of-flavor roast chicken.

Preheat the oven to 325°F (160°C). Season the chicken inside and out with salt and pepper and fill the cavity with most of the lemons and olives. Give it a good shake.

Take a very big cast-iron pot or other ovenproof casserole and put the potatoes in the bottom. Mix the oil with the rest of the lemons and olives and squash them a bit. Put the chicken in the pot on top of the potatoes and pour the oil and lemon mixture over it, letting the bits roll off onto the potatoes. Season well, then put the pot in the oven and shut the door. Let roast for at least 1½ hours.

Check the chicken is cooked by sticking a skewer between the legs and breast: If the juice that runs out is clear, the chicken is cooked. If not, put it back in the oven to continue roasting. You can also check for doneness with an instant-read thermometer, which should register 175–180°F (80–82°C).

When done, lift the chicken from the pot and pour all the bits from inside the cavity over the potatoes. Set the chicken on a carving board.

Place the pot over high heat and bring to a boil while you cut the chicken into big hunks. Return the chicken pieces to the pot along with any juices and take the pot to the table.

BEST-EVER ROAST CHICKEN

SERVES

handful of fresh sage leaves
handful of fresh marjoram
  sprigs
2 branches of fresh thyme,
  leaves picked from stems
½ cup soft butter
2 chickens, about 3 lb (1.4 kg)
  each
your choice of stuffing (pages
  164–168)
4 tbsp olive oil
6 large potatoes, peeled and
  cut into chunks
salt and black pepper

I am the biggest sucker for chicken. I am an even bigger sucker for chicken that has a good stuffing. For those who like to cook delicious food but keep it simple, this is a gem, because the potatoes, stuffing and chicken are all ready to eat at once, and the juices left behind make the best-ever gravy.

Preheat the oven to 350°F (175°C). Chop all the herbs roughly and mix them with the soft butter and some salt and pepper. Fill the neck end of the chickens with your preferred stuffing. Put one-third of the herb butter in the cavity of each chicken so the butter can melt inside the bird.

Place a high-sided roasting pan over high heat and add the oil. Drop in the potatoes and shake well to coat them in oil. Put the chickens in with the potatoes, pushing them out of the way. Place the roasting pan in the oven and let roast for 35 minutes, without opening the oven door.

Remove the pan from the oven and increase the temperature to 375°F (190°C). Turn the potatoes over and baste the birds well with the pan juices, spooning it generously over the breast. Return to the oven and roast for 40 minutes longer, at which point the chicken and potatoes should be done.

CARVING A ROAST BIRD

The secret to carving any bird is confidence plus a little understanding of how the bird is put together. You do have to practice, however, so roast a chicken every week and in three weeks you will be a master!

First, in your mind's eye, split the bird in half. Half a bird — be it chicken, duck, turkey or whatever — has from back to front a wing and wing joint, a breast and a leg (drumstick and thigh). Some people like the brown meat from the leg, and some like the white meat from the breast. Regardless of what you may think, the breast meat is the only part of the bird that needs to be sliced because anyone who likes the brown meat is very happy to gnaw on the bones.

Take the bird and, using a long, sharp knife, make a cut in between the thigh and the pointy end of the breast. Using the flat of the blade, push the leg away and let the skin tear naturally — the leg should just pop out and you will be left with a good amount of skin on the breast. Turn the bird around and cut between the wing and the fat end of the breast. Chop these bits any way you like — I separate the thigh from the drumstick and serve them to those whose hand is up quickest; I also separate the fat wing section from the pinions. The end bits are always mine, because they have lots of bones and delicious brown meat.

Now, if you do that on both sides of the bird you will be left with what in the professional kitchen we call the crown. Take long, thin slices of breast meat — use a long, thin knife and cut with confidence. If you leave too much meat on the bone, give the carcass to those who had their hand up for a leg and didn't get one. They will usually nibble on it happily.

CHICKEN GRAVY

The best gravy is always made in the roasting pan of the best roast chicken. To be successful you need to lift the chicken out when it has cooled a little, carefully draining any juices from inside it back into the pan. You can also prick the underside of the roast chicken a few times to drain out more of the good stuff.

Drain or spoon off most of the fat from the juices in the pan, but be sure to leave some fat. Set the roasting pan over medium heat and add 1½ tablespoons of flour. Stir well and let it cook for a few minutes, then add a couple of pinches of salt and a little pepper.

Add about 2 cups of water to the roasting pan, stirring well. Bring to a boil, scraping all the caramelized bits off the bottom of the pan and making sure there are no lumps. Add another 2 cups water and bring back to a boil. Cook for a few more minutes, stirring. Pour the gravy into a warmed pitcher. That's it. This is the first thing I learned to cook, aged five.

MASHED POTATOES

SERVES

4¹/₂ lb (2 kg) potatoes, peeled
¹/₂ cup butter
³/₄–1 cup milk
salt and white pepper

I think really good mash has to be beaten quite hard until it is creamy and peaky but still retaining the texture of a good floury potato. There are many theories about how mash should be prepared, so here I'm giving you some important basic principles. You can't really make hard-and-fast rules — you have to understand the feel of the cooked potato. I may well use only ¹/₂ cup of the milk and 2 tablespoons butter. If you start with a little of each you can add more, depending on how much the potato absorbs.

Cut the potatoes into equal-sized pieces so they will cook in the same amount of time. Put them in a pan and cover with plenty of cold salted water. Bring to a boil over medium heat, then cook gently so the water is just moving. When you can easily slip a knife through a potato, drain well. Return the potatoes to the pan and set it back on the heat to evaporate the excess moisture.

Mash the potatoes well with a masher or a fork (I prefer a fork but many do not). Keep the heat going under the pan to evaporate any moisture that may appear while the potatoes are being mashed. Season well, then start adding the butter, mixing it in roughly. Gradually add the milk, beating constantly over the heat until the mixture starts to bubble. Add more milk and butter as you like. If you want to add a touch of cream that is fine, although I prefer not to. Taste and season again. Serve with something as good and as simple.

BREAD SAUCE

SERVES

2 cups milk
1 medium onion, halved
6 black peppercorns
2 whole cloves
1 small blade mace, or a pinch
   of freshly grated nutmeg
2 cups fresh white bread
   crumbs
2 tbsp butter
sea salt

Once you have served your bread sauce, soak the pan in water, because the remains can set and be difficult to remove come dishwashing time.

Put the milk in a saucepan with the onion, spices and salt and set over medium heat. When the milk comes to a simmer, remove from the heat and let infuse for at least 15 minutes, or ideally for 1 hour. Strain and return to the pan.

Warm the milk again, then add the bread crumbs and butter, stirring well. Let the sauce cook for a few minutes. When ready, it should have body and thickness — a bit like oatmeal. If it is too thick, add a little more milk; if too thin, continue cooking until some liquid evaporates to give the desired consistency.

A QUICK RECIPE FOR CARROTS

SERVES

½ cup butter
12 small carrots, scrubbed
   or peeled
1 tsp brown sugar
salt and pepper

Melt the butter in a heavy pan, add ½ cup water and season well. Add the carrots and cook over medium heat until they have softened and the majority of the water has evaporated, about 10 minutes. Add the sugar, stir well and continue to cook until the sugar has dissolved, about 2 minutes.

GREEN PEA PUREE

SERVES

4 cups frozen green peas
3 green onions, chopped
4 tbsp butter
1/2 cup heavy cream

Put the peas in a medium-sized saucepan and cover with 1 cup boiling water. Place over high heat, add the green onions and butter and bring to a boil. Cook for 3 minutes. Add the cream and bring back to a boil.

Remove the pan from the heat. Blend the pea mixture in a food processor for 1 minute or so, until smooth.

TURKEY WITH CARAMELIZED ONIONS

SERVES

½ cup salted butter
2 tsp sea salt
2 tsp ground black pepper
1 turkey, about 10 lb (4.5 kg)
3 large onions

I wasn't particularly interested in turkey until I met award-winning British turkey farmer Paul Kelly and started to appreciate what this gem is all about, and why it is one of the United States' greatest exports, outside peanut butter. Make sure you have a roasting pan large enough to fit your turkey and a rack in the pan to set it on.

The night before roasting, soften the butter and add half the salt and half the pepper, mixing well. Remove the giblets from the bird and wipe it inside and out with paper towels.

Open the cavity of the bird and season the inside with the remaining salt and pepper. Rub the seasoned butter over the turkey. Take a piece of parchment paper twice the size of the breast and fold to give a double layer. Lay this over the breast (it will protect it during the cooking) and return the turkey to the refrigerator until the next morning.

Now calculate the roasting time — allow 20 minutes at the initial high temperature, then 30 minutes for every 2¼ lb (1 kg) after that. A 10 lb (4.5 kg) turkey will therefore take about 2½ hours to cook in total.

Preheat the oven to 425°F (220°C). Take the turkey from the refrigerator and let it come up to room temperature while the oven is heating.

Cut the onions in half and place in the roasting pan. Sit the turkey on a rack inside the pan. Carefully pour 1 cup hot water into the cavity of the bird, then close this with a skewer. Pour 2 cups of hot water into the roasting pan with the onions. Cover the whole thing with foil (I use two layers), making sure that it is well sealed around the edges.

Put the pan in the oven and roast for 20 minutes, then reduce the temperature to 400°F (200°C) and roast for the remaining cooking time. After 1½ hours, remove the foil and the parchment paper. Don't open the oven door again until the cooking time is up.

To test whether the turkey is cooked, insert a skewer or knife blade into the point where the thigh joins the breast. The juice should run clear; if it is pink, then roast the turkey for 20 minutes longer and test again. If you want to test for doneness with an instant-read thermometer, it should register 175–180°F (80–82°C).

Take the bird from the oven and let it rest in a warm place for at least 30 minutes. Strain the juice from the bottom of the roasting pan into a large pitcher to settle. The fat will rise to the top, leaving the aromatic turkey and onion juice beneath. Skim off the fat, then thicken the juices if you wish, or serve them as is.

Who is going to carve the turkey when it gets to the table, if indeed it gets that far? Well here are some helpful words from a very old edition of *Eliza Acton's Cookery and Household Management*: "A turkey does not call for greater skill in carving than a fowl. The first thing to do is to cut a succession of long slices from the breast, each with its nice little edge of untorn skin. The cutting of slices from the breast should begin as close to the wing as possible, and proceed upwards to the ridge of the breast bone."

She goes on to say: "The serving of the wings and the legs is only on rare occasions necessary at table, as the breast of the bird usually yields an ample supply for an average amount of guests. But in the event of the carver being called on to disjoint a wing or leg, it is done the same way as with a chicken."

STUFFING

4 tbsp butter

1 large onion, diced

$^1/_2$–$^3/_4$ cup roughly chopped
  bacon

2 cups finely chopped cooked
  chestnuts

2$^1/_2$ cups fresh bread crumbs

grated zest of 1 lemon

handful of fresh flat-leaf
  parsley, roughly chopped

salt and pepper

There are two schools of thought on stuffing. One is that the stuffing should be put inside the bird — and just in the neck end, near the wishbone, because putting it in the cavity lengthens the roasting time. The other is that the stuffing should be cooked separately (when it is sometimes called a dressing). Personally I agree with the latter, because the type of stuffing I prefer is quite dense and doesn't necessarily cook well inside the bird. Also, cooking the stuffing separately puts you in control of the cooking time, and results in crisp topping and sides and a lovely moist center. You can make this old-fashioned chestnut and bacon stuffing, and the ones on the following pages, the day before roasting.

In a frying pan, melt the butter over high heat and add a pinch of salt and two grinds from the pepper mill. Add the onion and cook until translucent. Add the bacon and cook for 5 minutes longer, stirring often so the onion doesn't burn.

Add the chestnuts, then remove from the heat. Mix in the bread crumbs, lemon zest and parsley. Taste and add more salt and pepper so that the stuffing is seasoned well.

Cook this stuffing and the ones on the following pages in the same way: Preheat the oven to 400°F (200°C). Grease a 12 x 4 inch (30 x 10 cm) baking dish and spoon in the stuffing (don't pat it down). Bake until hot and crisp on top, about 40 minutes, then serve with your roast bird.

PORK AND PEAR

2¼ lb (1 kg) pears, peeled
1½ cups white wine
2 cinnamon sticks
2 cloves
1 pork tenderloin, ground
finely grated zest of 1 lemon
3 heaped cups fresh bread crumbs
a few fresh sage leaves, chopped
2 juniper berries, crushed
1 egg

Put the pears, wine, cinnamon sticks and cloves in a saucepan and bring to a boil. Remove from the heat and let cool.

Drain the pears, reserving the cooking liquid, then chop them, discarding the cores and stalks. Mix with the rest of the ingredients, using a little of the pear cooking liquid to make it all moist, but bear in mind this mixture is supposed to be crumbly!

SPICED CRANBERRY AND APPLE

5 baking apples, peeled and chopped
2 cloves
¼ cup sugar
1 tsp red wine vinegar
1 bay leaf
3 cups frozen cranberries, thawed
2 large shallots, diced
2 garlic cloves, crushed
4 tbsp butter
1¼ cups ground turkey or chicken
1⅔ cups fresh bread crumbs, soaked in a little milk
1 egg
2 pinches of ground allspice
salt and pepper

Put the apples, cloves, sugar, vinegar and bay leaf in a saucepan and cook over low heat until soft but not mushy. Drop in the cranberries. Discard the cloves and bay leaf and set aside.

In another pan, cook the shallots and garlic in the butter until soft, then stir them into the ground turkey or chicken. Combine the two mixtures, then add the rest of the ingredients and mix well.

SAGE AND APPLE

2 large potatoes, peeled and chopped
2 onions, chopped
2 parsnips, peeled and chopped
4 tbsp butter
2 Granny Smith apples, peeled and chopped
handful of mixed chopped fresh sage and parsley
1 cup fresh bread crumbs
½ cup fresh bulk pork sausage
1 egg
salt and pepper

Cook the potatoes, onions and parsnips in boiling salted water until soft, then drain. Melt the butter in a pan, add the vegetables and fry for 1 minute. Season really well, adding lots of pepper. Stir in the apples and let cool. Then mix in all the rest of the ingredients. Taste and adjust the seasoning as you wish.

BOOZY RED CURRANT AND ORANGE

1 onion, diced
½ cup butter
½ cup chopped bacon
3 tbsp brandy or calvados
1 cup fresh bulk pork sausage
2½ cups fresh bread crumbs
2⅓ cups red currants
½ orange, zest and flesh chopped separately
finely grated zest of ½ lemon
small bunch of fresh parsley, minced
½ nutmeg, grated
1 egg
3–4 tbsp milk
salt and pepper

Soften the onion in the butter, then add the bacon and fry it quickly. Pour in the brandy and bring to a boil. Season well. Let cool, then mix the onion-bacon mixture with all the remaining ingredients to make a moist stuffing.

SAUSAGE AND HERB

1 garlic clove
1/2 cup cold water
1 onion, peeled
1 tbsp butter
1 apple, peeled and cored
1 2/3 cups fresh bread crumbs
2 1/4 lb (1 kg) fresh bulk pork sausage
small bunch of fresh parsley, leaves picked from stems
a few fresh sage leaves
salt and pepper

Crush the garlic to a paste with a little salt, then stir the paste into the cold water. Puree the onion in a food processor. Melt the butter in a frying pan and fry the pureed onion until tender.

Grate the apple in the food processor, then change back to the regular blade and add the bread crumbs, sausage, herbs and onion. Turn on to a high speed and as the motor runs pour the garlic-flavored water into the meat mixture. Season with pepper.

MIDDLE-EASTERN STYLE

2 shallots, diced
6 tbsp butter
1 1/4 cups ground chicken
6 fresh sage leaves, chopped
4 apples, cored and grated
10 dried apricots, soaked then finely chopped
2/3 cup toasted cashews
2/3 cup golden raisins
2 tbsp mixed, toasted ground cumin, cardamom
  and coriander
1 2/3 cups fresh bread crumbs, soaked in a little milk
1 egg
small bunch of cilantro, chopped
salt and pepper

Soften the shallots in 2 tablespoons butter, then season well. Let cool, then combine with the rest of the ingredients, including the remaining butter, in a large bowl. Mix well and slap it around the bowl until you have a firm paste that smells fragrant.

APPLE, SAGE AND CHESTNUT

1 1/2 tbsp butter
2 onions, diced
3 cups finely chopped cooked chestnuts
10 fresh sage leaves, torn, plus a few for garnish
1 2/3 cups fresh bread crumbs
1/2 cup water
3 Granny Smith apples, cored and grated
1 cup fresh bulk pork sausage
salt and pepper

Melt the butter in a pan and fry the onions over medium heat until translucent. Add the chestnuts and sage and season well. Cook for 2 minutes longer, then remove from the heat.

In a large bowl, soak the bread crumbs in the water until the water is all absorbed. Add the apples and sausage and beat well with a wooden spoon for about 3 minutes to incorporate some air (this will expand during cooking and give you a fluffy stuffing). Mix in the chestnuts and onions. Garnish with sage leaves when serving.

PRUNE AND CHESTNUT

2 large shallots, diced
2 garlic cloves, crushed
4 tbsp butter
6 celery stalks, finely chopped
1 cup chopped cooked chestnuts
1 cup port wine
2 handfuls of fresh flat-leaf parsley, chopped
1 1/2 cups fresh bulk pork sausage
salt and pepper
PRUNES IN ARMAGNAC
1 cup Agen prunes
2 Earl Grey teabags
pared zest and juice of 1 orange
1/2 cup Armagnac

Put the prunes in a bowl and add the teabags and orange zest and juice. Cover with boiling water. Let soak overnight. Drain, discarding the teabags and zest. Chop the prunes and mix with the Armagnac.

Soften the shallots and garlic in the butter. Season. Add the celery and chestnuts, raise the heat and cook for 2 minutes. Mix with the rest of the ingredients.

ROAST GROUSE WITH MADEIRA SAUCE

SERVES

4 small, young grouse
4 garlic cloves
4 fresh sage leaves
salt and pepper
4 handfuls of watercress,
  for serving

SAUCE
grouse wings, necks and
  giblets, chopped
olive oil
1 shallot, chopped
6 mushrooms, chopped
1 carrot, chopped
1 celery stalk, chopped
1 garlic clove, chopped
½ cup Madeira
1 cup chicken stock (page 20)
1 cup meat stock, preferably
  veal stock
2 fresh sage leaves

Because grouse is not farmed, what you buy in the market will be imported. For roasting, you want young grouse weighing about 1 lb (450 g) each, to serve one per person. Ask your butcher to take the wings and necks off the birds, but to give these to you with the giblets so you can use them for the sauce.

Start with the sauce (it can be made the day before serving, if preferred). In a wide pan, fry the wings and necks in a bit of olive oil until golden brown. Drain off the excess fat, then add the chopped vegetables and garlic. Cook for 1 minute. Add the Madeira, bring to a boil and reduce to a syrupy consistency. Add the chicken stock and boil until reduced by half, then add the meat stock and reduce again until you have a light sauce.

Chop the giblets and season them. Add to the sauce to enrich it. Bring the sauce to a boil once more, then press through a fine sieve. Add the sage leaves and keep warm until serving (or let cool if making in advance).

To cook the grouse, preheat the oven to 400°F (200°C) and put a roasting pan in it to get hot. Place one garlic clove and a sage leaf in each bird, then season inside and out. Heat a large frying pan with a little oil over high heat and sear the birds all over until golden. Transfer them to the roasting pan and add a little more oil. Roast for 8 minutes, basting frequently with the fat in the pan. Remove from the oven and let rest for a minute.

Reheat the sauce if necessary, and serve with the grouse.

GAME CHIPS

SERVES

4 large potatoes
2 quarts (8 cups) vegetable oil
salt

These are of course potato chips, but we call them game chips because they are so good with roast game birds. Another name for them is Saratoga chips. To make them at home it is helpful to have a mandoline, or a mandoline-style slicing attachment for your food processor. You only need a few chips for each serving, which is a good thing, because once you start cooking them they quickly disappear.

Slice the potatoes very thinly — so thin that if held up to the light it will shine through. Fill a sink or bowl with cold water and rinse the sliced potatoes. Change the water and repeat until the water stays clear, indicating that most of the starch has been removed.

Heat the oil to 375°F (190°C) in a deep-fryer with a basket.

Working in batches, gently place each potato slice in the oil as if you were the dealer at a card game. Fry for 3 minutes, then stir well so that the chips do not stick together (if they are sticking, the oil may not be hot enough, or the potato has not been thoroughly rinsed of starch). Continue frying and stirring the chips for 8–10 minutes.

Remove the chips from the oil and drain well on paper towels. Repeat with the remaining potatoes. Place the chips in a brown paper bag while still warm and sprinkle with salt.

PHEASANT WRAPPED IN PROSCIUTTO WITH POLENTA

SERVES

8 slices prosciutto
16 fresh sage leaves
8 pheasant breasts, excess
   fat trimmed
1/2 cup butter
3 tbsp olive oil
juice of 1 large lemon
flaky sea salt and pepper

POLENTA
1 1/4 cups milk
1 garlic clove, crushed
1/4 tsp salt
1/2 tsp ground black pepper
3/4 cup polenta
1/2 cup heavy cream
1/3 cup freshly grated
   Parmesan cheese
1/3 cup mascarpone

Lay two slices of prosciutto side by side and slightly overlapping. Place a sage leaf in the middle. Lay a pheasant breast on top, skin-side down. Season well. Place a couple of sage leaves on the meat side, then add a good nugget of butter. Lay a second breast on top, skin-side up, to make a sandwich. Place another sage leaf on top of that breast and carefully fold the prosciutto over the breasts, wrapping tightly. Repeat with the remaining prosciutto and pheasant. This operation can be done the day before serving; the sage flavors the meat a little more when left for some time.

To make the polenta, put 1 cup water in a saucepan with the milk, garlic, salt and pepper and bring to a rolling boil. Rain in the polenta, stirring constantly in a clockwise direction, and keep stirring until the mixture thickens and comes back to a boil. Reduce the heat to very low and cook, stirring very frequently, for 45 minutes. Add the cream and Parmesan, then continue cooking over low heat for 10 minutes. Remove the pan from the heat and stir the mascarpone into the polenta. Let cool for 10 minutes before serving.

Meanwhile, preheat the oven to 400°F (200°C). Heat a heavy frying pan over high heat. Pour a little oil into the hot pan and add the wrapped breasts. Let cook until the edges start to brown, about 3 minutes, then turn them over and cook for 3 minutes longer. Transfer the wrapped breasts to a small roasting pan and place in the oven to finish cooking for 8 minutes, watching to be sure they don't get too brown.

Set the pheasant breasts aside and put the pan juices over low heat. Stir in the remaining butter and the lemon juice to make a sauce. Serve the pheasant with the polenta and sauce.

ROAST PARTRIDGE WITH POTATOES AND ROSEMARY

SERVES

1 cup butter
4¹/₂ lb (2 kg) large potatoes,
   peeled and thinly sliced
3 cups sliced white onions
1 cup strong chicken or game
   stock (pages 20–21)
8 partridges
large handful of fresh sage
10 branches of fresh rosemary
vegetable oil
salt and pepper

Boulangère potatoes flavored with rosemary, with the juices of roast partridges dripping into them — yum!

Preheat the oven to 350°F (175°C). Grease a large baking dish with plenty of butter. Mix the sliced potatoes and onions with plenty of salt and pepper, then add the stock. Pour into the buttered dish and pat it all down. Bake for 40 minutes.

Meanwhile, rub the partridges with some more of the butter, season well and stuff the cavities with sage. Rub the rosemary branches with oil and salt.

When the potatoes have been cooking for 40 minutes, raise the heat to 400°F (200°C) and lay half the rosemary on the potatoes. Sit the birds on top and cover with the rest of the rosemary. Return to the oven and roast for 20 minutes longer.

Take the potatoes and partridges from the oven and serve. You can't eat the rosemary, but it smells so beautiful, so just take the dish to the table and listen to the enthusiastic welcome.

FIVE-SPICED CHINESE DUCK WITH BOK CHOY AND OYSTER SAUCE

SERVES

DUCK

1 large duck
3/4 cup sugar
pinch of sea salt
6 star anise
5-inch (12.5 cm) piece of fresh
   ginger, peeled and sliced
small bunch of green onions,
   roughly chopped
2 tbsp maltose syrup
2¹/₂ tbsp red wine vinegar

BOK CHOY

4 tbsp fish sauce
14 oz (400 g) bok choy, halved
   lengthwise
4 tbsp oyster sauce
1 fresh, long red chili, thinly
   sliced at an angle
cilantro leaves, for garnish

I usually roast two ducks at a time and then freeze one for another day.

Two days before serving, wash the duck inside and out with cold water, then drain and pat dry. Mix together the sugar, salt, star anise, ginger and green onions. Fill the cavity with this, then secure it closed with a wooden skewer (soaked in water first).

Mix the maltose and 2 tablespoons of the vinegar with 1 tablespoon of boiling water and set aside. Fill a big pitcher with boiling water, add the remaining vinegar and pour over the duck. The boiling water opens up the pores, while the vinegar helps strip some of the waxiness from the skin so it will be more receptive to the maltose. Smear the maltose mixture over the duck, then hang it up in a cool place to dry overnight.

Preheat the oven to 425°F (220°C). Put a little water in the bottom of a roasting pan and set the duck on a rack in the pan. Roast for 45 minutes. Carefully lift the duck off the rack and drain off the water and fat from the pan. Return the duck to the rack and continue roasting until the duck is well done, about 40 minutes (there is no such thing as rare Chinese roast duck). Take the duck from the oven and let it sit for about 20 minutes. (You can let it cool completely, then wrap and freeze at this point.)

Take the meat off the carcass and reserve it. Put all the duck bones in a pot with 4 cups water and the fish sauce. Bring to a boil and simmer for 5 minutes. Add the bok choy halves and cook for 1–2 minutes, then lift them out. Reserve the broth.

Divide the bok choy among four serving bowls. Swirl some oyster sauce around. Cut up the duck so that each person gets some leg and breast meat on top of the vegetables. Sprinkle with chili, spoon over a little of the broth and garnish with cilantro leaves.

Tip: I am a great believer in intensifying flavor any way you can, so before roasting Chinese duck I often put some sugar, spices and green onions inside, which adds enormously to the flavor and also helps to tenderize the meat.

GOOSE AND MUSTARD FRUITS
WITH MARSALA SAUCE

SERVES 🦃 🦃 🦃 🦃

1 goose, about 7½ lb (3.5 kg)
1 head garlic
3 sprigs of fresh thyme
3 sprigs of fresh rosemary
2 onions, halved (skin on)
6 slices bacon
mostarda di Cremona (mustard
  fruit chutney), for serving
salt and pepper

MARSALA SAUCE
2 shallots, chopped
12 juniper berries, crushed
a little olive oil
½ cup brandy
²/₃ cup marsala
²/₃ cup Madeira
1 cup your choice of poultry
  or meat stock

**I like my roast goose to be almost falling off the bone.
The meat can be used cold the next day in a salad.**

Clean the goose inside and out, trim off any excess fat and season
inside and out. Put the garlic, thyme and rosemary in the cavity
with ½ cup water. Refrigerate until 2 hours before roasting.

Preheat the oven to 425°F (220°C). Set the goose on a rack in a
roasting pan and pour in 1½ cups water. Place the unpeeled onion
halves, cut-side up, around the bird and lay the bacon slices over
the breast. Cover the whole thing with foil, sealing it well, and
roast for 1 hour.

Take the goose from the oven and remove the foil. Reduce the heat
to 400°F (200°C) and roast uncovered for 1 hour longer, basting
twice with the pan juices.

Meanwhile, start the sauce. Sweat the shallots and juniper berries
in a little oil until soft. Add all the alcohol and flame carefully.
Pour in the stock, bring to a boil and reduce to a saucelike
consistency. Strain and set aside.

When the goose is cooked, let it rest for 15 minutes. Drain the pan
juices into a bowl and set aside. Put the pan on medium heat and
turn the onions cut side down to cook for a few minutes so they
soak up the flavors.

When the pan juices have separated, skim off and discard the fat.
Open the goose slightly and drain the liquid out of the cavity into
the bowl. Add with the marsala sauce to the roasting pan and
bring to a boil. Reduce until the sauce starts to thicken, then
strain it and season to taste.

Meanwhile, return the bird to the oven for 15 minutes to crisp the
skin. Serve with the marsala sauce and *mostarda*.

GUINEA FOWL WITH SWEET POTATOES

SERVES

½ cup butter, plus 1 tbsp extra

1 tsp smoked paprika

2 large sweet potatoes

1 large guinea fowl — at least
  2¼ lb (1 kg)

juice of 1 lemon, plus the
  chopped squeezed lemon

1 onion, chopped

4 black peppercorns, crushed

1 branch of fresh rosemary

1½ tbsp olive oil

4 large shallots, quartered
  lengthwise

about 1 cup plain yogurt

1 tsp sumac (optional)

toasted flatbreads, for serving

salt and pepper

Mix the butter and smoked paprika together. Peel the sweet potatoes and halve each one lengthwise, then cut each half into four hunks.

Preheat the oven to 400°F (200°C). Remove the innards from the guinea fowl, wash it well inside, and dry. Fill the cavity with the chopped lemon, onion, crushed peppercorns, some salt and the rosemary. Season the outside of the bird with salt and pepper, then brush the flavored butter all over the front and legs.

Set an ovenproof casserole over high heat. Add the extra 1 tablespoon butter with the oil, and once sizzling cook the sweet potatoes and shallots for 5 minutes. Put the bird in the casserole and give the pot a good shake, then transfer to the oven. Roast for 1 hour, basting the bird and vegetables frequently.

Remove from the oven and let the bird rest for 5 minutes before carving. Stir the lemon juice into the yogurt, place in a serving bowl and sprinkle with the sumac. Serve the guinea fowl with the vegetables and pan juices as gravy, with the yogurt and toasted flatbreads on the side.

If you haven't worked it out yet, then I am about to tell you: I am actually quite a lazy cook. Well, not really lazy, but I don't believe in being a slave to the kitchen. Entertaining, feeding the family and eating well are all things I love to do, but I don't feel I have to spend hours in the kitchen to get a great result.

The one-pot wonder is an antidote for the busy person who loves to cook but has guilt trips about eating good food if time is limited. I say, don't worry. Make sure you are careful and always use great produce, but just put it all in the pot and walk away, to do whatever else needs to be done.

One-pot wonders are meant to be a centerpiece that everyone dives into, taking the bits they like and leaving the bits they don't, sharing great food and great conversation. Honestly, this is one of the most enjoyable ways to cook. Take your time with the shopping and then, when you get home, prepare the dinner, lunch or even brunch without much effort.

one-pot wonders

HEARTY CHICKEN CASSEROLE WITH DUMPLINGS

SERVES

3 tbsp all-purpose flour

6 chicken breast halves (bone in), each cut into 3 pieces

7 tbsp vegetable oil

12 oz (340 g) boiling onions, peeled, or 4 medium onions, peeled and each cut into 8

7 oz (200 g) slab bacon, cut into cubes

3 garlic cloves, crushed

3 large carrots, peeled and cut into chunks

10 oz (285 g) open cremini mushrooms, sliced

2 large potatoes, peeled and diced

2 bay leaves

2 tbsp red-currant jelly

1^1/$_2$ cups red wine

1^1/$_4$ cups chicken stock (page 20)

salt and pepper

DUMPLINGS

5 oz (140 g) finely chopped beef suet (from a butcher)

2^1/$_3$ cups self-rising flour

about ^{2}/$_3$ cup warm water

Preheat the oven to 400°F (200°C). Put the flour in a plastic bag and season with lots of salt and pepper. Drop the chicken into the flour and shake vigorously to coat well.

Heat the oil in a large ovenproof casserole and brown the chicken pieces over high heat. Remove the chicken and reduce the heat. Add the onions and bacon and cook until they are colored and smell good, 5–8 minutes. Add the garlic and then the carrots, mushrooms, potatoes, bay leaves and red-currant jelly. Stir well. Put the chicken back in and stir to coat well. Pour in the wine and stock. Cover and bring to a boil, then transfer the pot to the oven to cook for 40 minutes.

To make the dumplings, combine the suet, flour and a big pinch of salt in a mixing bowl. Gradually stir in the warm water, mixing to give a heavy dough. Roll the mixture into balls about the size of a golf ball. Take the casserole from the oven. Drop in the dumplings, cover again and return to the oven for a final 20 minutes of cooking.

COQ AU VIN

SERVES

2 chickens, each cut into 8, or
16 chicken parts
about ½ cup butter
24 shallots, peeled
7 oz (200 g) pancetta or slab
bacon, cubed
3 garlic cloves, squashed
3 cups full-bodied red wine
3 cups sliced button
mushrooms
large handful of chopped
fresh parsley
salt and pepper

Celebrated British food writer Elizabeth David cooked her chicken whole, then caramelized onions in butter and sugar and added them to the pot at the end of cooking. Other people prefer to use cut-up chicken and add mushrooms for the last few minutes. Some think you should use a tough stewing chicken, others a younger, plumper bird. My view is that it is important to use a chicken with quite a bit of fat in it, not a scrawny thing, and not to kill the texture by overcooking it. This is a two-chicken recipe for eight or 10 people, so if you are cooking for fewer then halve it.

Preheat the oven to 400°F (200°C). Season the chicken pieces generously. Heat 4 tablespoons of the butter in an ovenproof casserole and fry the chicken with half the shallots and half the bacon. When everything is colored, add the garlic and wine. Bring to a boil, then cover tightly and transfer to the oven. Cook until the chicken is done, 1–1½ hours.

In a frying pan, cook the remaining shallots with 4 tablespoons butter and ½ cup water. When the water has evaporated the shallots will be soft. Add the rest of the bacon along with the mushrooms, plus some more butter if needed. Season with lots of ground pepper and a little salt. Toss until the bacon and mushrooms are just golden, then tip them into the casserole. Add the chopped parsley and serve.

POT AU FEU

SERVES 🐔🐔🐔🐔🐔🐔

1 chicken, about 5½ lb (2.5 kg)
1½ cups white wine
4 large shallots
1 bouquet garni, made with
   3 bay leaves, 3 thyme sprigs,
   2 celery stalks, and 3 cloves
4 carrots, peeled and chopped
2 leeks, chopped
20 new potatoes, peeled
1 small head celery root,
   peeled and chopped

DUMPLINGS

5 oz (140 g) finely chopped
   beef suet (from a butcher)
2⅓ cups self-rising flour
large handful of chopped
   fresh parsley
⅔ cup warm water

STUFFING

1 cup fresh bulk pork sausage
⅔ cup diced slab bacon
3–4 chicken livers, chopped
   (optional)
3 fresh sage leaves, chopped
1 egg
2 garlic cloves, chopped
4 large shallots, diced
bunch of fresh flat-leaf parsley,
   chopped
2 large handfuls of fresh
   bread crumbs
salt and pepper

Preheat the oven to 375°F (190°C). To make the stuffing, put all the ingredients in a bowl and mix to a paste.

Trim excess fat from the chicken cavity, then fill with the stuffing. Close each end of the bird with a couple of big skewers. Put the chicken in an ovenproof casserole. Add the wine, shallots, bouquet garni and some salt and pepper. Pour in enough water to rise one knuckle above the bird, then cover and place in the oven to cook for 1½ hours.

Take the casserole from the oven and add the carrots, leeks, potatoes and celery root, being careful not to move the chicken too much. Return to the oven to cook for 30 minutes longer.

To make the dumplings, mix the suet, flour, parsley and a big pinch of salt in a large bowl. Stir in the warm water to make a heavy dough. Roll the mixture into balls the size of a golf ball.

Remove the pot from the oven again. Lift out the chicken, put it on a plate, cover tightly and set aside. Leave all the vegetables in the pot. Add the dumplings and set over high heat. Bring to a boil, then reduce to a simmer and cook for 15 minutes.

Take the skin off the chicken and discard it. Cut up the meat and the stuffing and keep them warm. Heat your serving bowls. Divide the chicken, stuffing, vegetables and dumplings among the bowls, spoon the pan juices over, and serve with mustard and crusty bread.

BRAISED GUINEA FOWL WITH CELERY ROOT AND CRISP BACON

SERVES 🐔🐔🐔🐔🐔🐔🐔🐓🐓

10 oz (285 g) slab bacon or
  pancetta, cut into thick
  chunks
2 guinea fowl, each cut into
  8 pieces
²/₃ cup all-purpose flour
2 onions, sliced
1 lemon, halved
2 bay leaves
handful of dried mushrooms
10 garlic cloves
1³/₄ cups chicken stock
  (page 20)
3¹/₂ tbsp white or red wine
  vinegar
1 lb (450 g) celery root (also
  called celeriac), peeled and
  cut into hunks the same size
  as the guinea fowl pieces
small bunch of cilantro, leaves
  picked from stems
bunch of fresh tarragon,
  chopped
salt and pepper

These birds are cooked in rendered bacon fat and the crisp bacon is saved to be scattered on top. For this you will need thick chunks of bacon, or pancetta, which is the Italian equivalent.

Preheat the oven to 350°F (175°C). Drop the bacon into a large, cold ovenproof casserole and set it over high heat. As it heats, the fat will melt and the bacon will start to fry. Once colored and crisp, add some salt and pepper. Remove the bacon with a slotted spoon and set aside on paper towels. Reduce the heat under the casserole to medium.

Dust the guinea fowl pieces in the flour and, in batches, add them to the casserole and color on all sides. Return all the pieces to the pot. Add the onions, lemon, bay leaves, dried mushrooms and garlic and let them color for a few minutes. Add the stock, vinegar and celery root, stir well and bring to a boil.

Transfer to the oven to cook uncovered for 45 minutes. Just before serving, heat the bacon in a frying pan. Scatter over the casserole along with the cilantro and tarragon. Serve with mustard.

GUINEA FOWL TAGINE

SERVES

1 guinea fowl

a little olive oil

2 carrots, cut into chunks

2 red onions, cut into chunks

6 prunes, dates or dried figs

rind of 1 preserved lemon, cut into strips

sprig of fresh mint, leaves chopped

harissa, for serving

CHERMOULA

1 large red onion, roughly chopped

1 large garlic clove

5/8-inch (1.5 cm) piece of fresh ginger, roughly chopped

7 tbsp olive oil

7 tbsp lemon juice

1/2 tsp Thai fish sauce

1 heaped tsp honey

1/2 tsp ground cumin

1/2 tsp paprika

1/2 tsp ground turmeric

1/2 tsp hot chili powder

handful each of fresh flat-leaf parsley and cilantro

COUSCOUS

1/2 cup couscous

1 tsp salt

7 tbsp butter, cubed

small handful of golden raisins

I really hope that no one who tries this dish portions it up neatly in the kitchen and then takes it to the table. This is intended to be wonderful put-the-pot-in-the-middle-of-the-table food.

The day before cooking, put all the ingredients for the chermoula in a blender and mix until smooth. Pour this over the bird and let marinate in the refrigerator overnight.

Next day, preheat the oven to 425°F (220°C). Heat a little olive oil in a large frying pan and brown the guinea fowl on all sides over high heat. Put the carrots, onions and fruit into a tagine or ovenproof casserole and place the guinea fowl on top. Pour in about 1¾ cups water — enough to come ½ inch (1.2 cm) from the top of the casserole. Cover and cook in the oven for about 45 minutes. Turn the heat down to 350°F (175°C) and cook for another 45 minutes.

About 15 minutes before serving, rinse the couscous in cold water and put in a shallow bowl. Season with salt and scatter the butter and raisins over. Pour on enough boiling water to cover the couscous by about ½ inch (1.2 cm). Cover and leave until the grains are plump and tender, about 10 minutes.

Open the tagine at the table and scatter the preserved lemon and mint over. Serve the couscous and harissa separately.

Variation: you can use this recipe for whole chicken or lamb shanks, but increase the cooking time to 3 hours. For squabs, reduce it to 1 hour. In each case, lower the temperature halfway through the cooking time.

SQUABS IN A POT

SERVES

olive oil
4 squabs
7 oz (200 g) slab bacon or
   pancetta, cut into pieces
2 oz (55 g) dried porcini
1 head savoy cabbage, cut
   into chunks
18 fresh sage leaves
1/2 cup butter
squeeze of lemon juice
salt and pepper

Preheat the oven to 425°F (220°C). Heat a little oil in a large ovenproof casserole. Season the squabs, then put them into the pot and cook until browned all over. Remove and keep warm. Add the bacon or pancetta, dried porcini, cabbage and about two-thirds of the sage to the pot. Toss until the bacon and vegetables color.

Set the squabs on top of the bacon and cabbage mixture. Add the butter, then cover the pot and transfer to the oven. Cook for about 30 minutes — when done the breast meat should remain a bit pink but the leg meat will come easily away from the bone.

Squeeze on the lemon juice and scatter the rest of the sage over. Great with boiled potatoes and mustard.

DUCK WITH OLIVES AND VINEGAR SAUCE

SERVES

3 tbsp all-purpose flour
1 tsp flaky sea salt
$^1/_2$ tsp white pepper
1 duck, cut into 8 pieces
7 tbsp olive oil
1$^1/_2$ tbsp butter
7 tbsp cabernet sauvignon
  vinegar
2 tbsp white wine
1 cup pitted black olives
4 shallots, roughly chopped
1 garlic clove, chopped
3 bay leaves
2 branches of fresh rosemary,
  leaves picked from stems

Make sure you use a good smooth-tasting cabernet sauvignon vinegar for this. If you want to use sherry vinegar instead, or your vinegar tastes sharp, reduce the quantity to 4 tablespoons.

Preheat the oven to 325°F (160°C). Season the flour with sea salt and white pepper and dust the duck pieces in it. Heat a small amount of the olive oil with the butter in an ovenproof casserole. Add the duck and brown all over. Add the remaining olive oil, the vinegar, wine, olives, shallots, garlic and bay leaves. Give the ingredients a good shuffle, then let cook for 5–8 minutes to give the shallots some color.

Add the rosemary, then cover the casserole and transfer to the oven. Cook for 1 hour 20 minutes. Serve with mashed potatoes (page 157).

SLOW-ROAST PHEASANTS, BARLEY AND WILD MUSHROOMS

SERVES

3/4 cup butter

4 tbsp vegetable oil

2 large pheasants

7 oz (200 g) wild mushrooms

4 portobello mushrooms, chopped roughly

3 large onions, quartered

1 cup pearl barley

6 cups chicken or game stock (pages 20–21)

handful of small watercress sprigs

salt and pepper

"Slowly, slowly" they say with barley, which is true here — this meaty little number needs time in the oven. It will all be soft and delicious, with the breasts of the pheasants still moist and succulent.

Preheat the oven to 325°F (160°C). Melt 7 tablespoons of the butter with the oil in an ovenproof casserole. Season the pheasants, then brown them all over. Remove from the pot. Fry the wild mushrooms in the fat left in the pot, then lift them out with a slotted spoon. Put the chopped mushrooms and onions into the casserole and fry them well. Stir in the barley.

Return the pheasants to the pot and push them down so they sink into the barley. Sprinkle the wild mushrooms over the top, then pour in the stock and bring to a boil. Cover and transfer to the oven to cook for at least 1 hour.

Take the casserole from the oven and check to see if the barley is done. Take the pheasants out and set aside. Give the barley a good stir and add the remaining butter. Taste and season as necessary.

Break the pheasants up using your hands or a knife and fork — they should come apart easily. Serve the pheasant on the barley, with watercress scattered over.

I am going to be controversial: the Australians make the best pies in the world. Sorry, but it is true. When I say pie, I mean the sort you hold in your hands to eat, letting the filling dribble down your chin and between your fingers. So, as an Australian, I am proud to present to you a few inspiring pies and tarts, the latter being fancier pies without a lid.

Some of my all-time favorites, of which I am very proud, are also in here, such as the curry puff made with leftover chicken or turkey. We always had this the day after Christmas and on Easter Monday (it just goes to show how expensive chicken was when I was a kid; we only had it on special occasions). I've also included that other 1970s' favorite: the vol-au-vent.

The pies in this chapter vary from a classic British game pie with hot-water pastry to the great American pot pie. All these recipes are meant to inspire. Who ate all the pies? I did, and loved every single one.

savory pies

CHICKEN POT PIE

SERVES

13/4 lb (800 g) boneless
   chicken thighs and breast
   halves, halved
1 cup chicken stock (page 20)
1/2 cup light cream or creamy
   milk
6 celery stalks, chopped
2 leeks, cut into 1/2-inch
   (1.2 cm) pieces
8 oz (225 g) new potatoes,
   halved crosswise
4 garlic cloves, chopped
1 lb (450 g) cooked ham, cut
   into 1-inch (2.5 cm) cubes
4 tbsp butter
6 tbsp all-purpose flour
1/2 tsp freshly grated nutmeg
1/4 cup chopped fresh flat-leaf
   parsley
1 sheet frozen puff pastry,
   thawed
1 egg yolk beaten with 1 tbsp
   milk, for glazing
salt and pepper

Put the chicken, stock, cream, celery, leeks, potatoes, garlic and ham in a large saucepan. Bring to a boil, then reduce the heat, cover and simmer until the chicken is tender, 20–25 minutes.

Set a colander over a large bowl and pour the contents of the pan into it. Measure the liquid in the bowl: you need 2 cups, so discard any extra or add more cream or milk.

Clean and dry the pan. Add the butter and melt over medium heat. Stir in the flour until bubbling, but do not let the mixture color. Add the reserved liquid about one-third at a time, stirring well until thick and smooth. Stir in the nutmeg and parsley, then season to taste. Add the contents of the colander and toss gently in the sauce until well coated. Let cool for 10 minutes. (You can make the filling in advance up to this point and refrigerate.)

Preheat the oven to 400°F (200°C). Lay out the sheet of puff pastry on the work surface. Put a 5-cup baking dish that is 3 inches (7.5 cm) deep upside down on the pastry. Cut around it, with an extra 1½-inch (3.8 cm) border. Also cut a strip of pastry ¾ inch (2 cm) wide to fit around the rim of the dish. Brush the rim with water and stick the strip onto it.

Ladle the filling into the dish, piling it up high in the center. Moisten the pastry strip, then set the pastry lid on top of the dish and press to seal to the strip. Trim off any excess pastry. Cut a little slit in the center, then brush the egg glaze over the pastry. Mark a decorative pattern in the pastry, if desired.

Bake until the pastry has puffed, about 25 minutes, then reduce the temperature to 350°F (175°C) and continue baking until the pastry is crusty and golden, about 15 minutes. (If you made the filling in advance and it was cold when you put it in the oven, continue cooking for 30 minutes longer.) If the pastry is browning too much, cover it with a folded sheet of damp parchment paper. Serve hot, straight from the dish.

CHICKEN, LEEK AND MUSHROOM POT PIE

SERVES

½ cup butter

2 leeks, cut into ½-inch
   (1.2 cm) pieces

6 celery stalks, chopped

⅓ cup all-purpose flour, plus
   6 tbsp extra

1 cup chicken stock (page 20)

½ cup light cream

7 oz (200 g) button mushrooms

1¾ lb (800 g) roast chicken
   meat without skin or bone,
   cubed or shredded (about
   5½ cups)

¼ cup chopped fresh flat-leaf
   parsley

1 sheet frozen puff pastry,
   thawed

1 egg yolk beaten with 1 tbsp
   milk, for glazing

salt and pepper

Melt half of the butter in a large saucepan, add the leeks and celery and cook for 5 minutes, stirring constantly. Add ⅓ cup flour and mix to a paste. Stir in the stock and cream. Bring to a boil, then reduce the heat, cover and simmer for 15 minutes. Remove from the heat and add the mushrooms and chicken. Season and add the parsley

Preheat the oven to 425°F (220°C). Lay out the sheet of puff pastry on the work surface. Put a 5-cup baking dish that is 3 inches (7.5 cm) deep upside down on the pastry. Cut around it, with an extra 1½-inch (3.8 cm) border. Also cut a strip of pastry ¾ inch (2 cm) wide to fit around the rim of the dish. Brush the rim with water and stick the strip onto it.

Ladle the filling into the dish, piling it up high in the center. Moisten the pastry strip, then set the pastry lid on top of the dish and press to seal to the strip. Cut a small slit in the center of the lid, then brush with the egg glaze. Mark a decorative pattern in the pastry, if desired.

Bake for 25 minutes, then reduce the temperature to 400°F (200°C) and bake until the pastry is crusty and golden, about 15 minutes longer. If the pastry browns too quickly, cover it with a folded sheet of damp parchment paper. Serve hot, straight from the dish.

"RAISED" CHICKEN AND PARTRIDGE PIE

SERVES

FILLING

2¼ lb (1 kg) chicken, skinned, boned and cut into thumb-sized chunks (keep all the trimmings)

1 lb (450 g) pork shoulder, boned and coarsely ground (keep all the trimmings)

1 bay leaf

8 partridge breasts

2 tsp salt

2 tsp cayenne pepper

1 tsp ground white pepper

1 tsp ground black pepper

4 tbsp sherry

3 hard-boiled egg yolks

1 tsp unflavored granulated gelatin

HOT-WATER PASTRY

6 tbsp lard

2 cups all-purpose flour

1 tsp salt

1 egg, beaten, for glazing

If you have a beautiful fluted oval mold, use it for this traditional British pie, which is served cold.

First take all the poultry and pork trimmings and put them in a large saucepan with the bay leaf. Cover with water, bring to a boil and let simmer for 3 hours.

Meanwhile, combine the salt and spices in a bowl and stir in the sherry. Mix the chicken, partridge and pork together on a work surface, then push the mixture out flat. Pour over the spiced sherry and roll it all together, mixing well.

To make the pastry, put the lard in a saucepan with 5 tablespoons water and bring to a boil. Sift the flour and salt together twice into a large bowl. Add the hot liquid and stir vigorously until combined. Cover the bowl with a dish towel.

Preheat the oven to 350°F (175°C). Take three-quarters of the warm pastry and roll it out to ½-inch (1.2 cm) thickness. Use to line the mold and trim away the excess. Half-fill the case with the meat mixture. Make three indentations down the middle and insert the egg yolks. Top with the rest of the meat, piling it up a little above the top of the mold.

Roll out the remaining pastry to make the lid. Rub the rim of the pie shell with water and press on the lid. Crimp the edges so the pie is well sealed. Brush with egg and decorate with the pastry trimmings. Cut a slit in the center of the lid. Bake for 30 minutes, then reduce the temperature to 300°F (150°C) and continue baking for 2 hours. Remove the pie from the oven and let cool.

Meanwhile, strain the stock and measure 1 cup. Stir in the gelatin and season well. When the pie is at room temperature, use a funnel to pour the stock into the pie through the slit. Chill for at least 2 hours, or preferably overnight, before serving.

CHICKEN OR TURKEY VOL-AU-VENTS

MAKES

2 sheets frozen puff pastry, thawed

1 egg beaten with a little milk, for glazing

²/₃ cup sliced button mushrooms

2 tsp butter, plus extra for greasing

2 heaped cups diced cooked chicken or turkey

1 cup thick béchamel sauce

dry bread crumbs

salt and pepper

These may seem old-fashioned, but they are a real classy way to use up leftovers. I love the thick, creamy mushroom sauce with bits of chicken or turkey. If you don't want to make the vol-au-vent cases you can use bought patty shells to hold the creamed poultry.

Preheat the oven to 400°F (200°C). Lay the pastry sheets on the work surface and use a cutter or glass to cut out 24 disks. Place half the disks on a greased baking sheet and brush them with the egg glaze. Using a smaller cutter than the first one, cut holes from the center of the remaining pastry disks so that you have 12 rings. Lay the rings on top of the disks on the baking sheet. Use a fork to prick holes in the bases of the vol-au-vent shells.

Bake until golden and risen but not crisp, about 20 minutes. You should be able to push down the centers of the vol-au-vent shells easily, to make room for the filling.

While the pastry shells are baking, gently fry the mushrooms in the butter. Season well and remove from the heat. Stir in the chicken or turkey, then pour in the béchamel and mix well.

Spoon some filling into each vol-au-vent shell, then sprinkle with bread crumbs. Put back into the oven to bake for 15 minutes longer, then serve hot.

CURRY PUFFS

MAKES

2 cups shredded cooked
   chicken or turkey
½ cup thick curry sauce
   (bought is fine)
⅓ cup frozen green peas,
   thawed
2 sheets frozen puff pastry,
   thawed
milk, for glazing
butter, for greasing

This is one of the best ways to use up leftover turkey or chicken. The puffs should be quite small — a two-bite size is just right.

Mix the chicken or turkey, curry sauce and peas together and set aside.

Lay out the pastry on the work surface and cut out 20 disks 2½–3 inches (6.3–7.5 cm) in diameter. Brush the disks lightly with milk. Put a heaped teaspoon of the curry mixture in the middle of each disk and fold into a crescent shape. Pick each one up and push the edges together to seal well.

Place the puffs on a greased baking sheet. When they are all filled and lined up, brush each one with more milk. Refrigerate for at least an hour, or up to a day.

When ready to cook, preheat the oven to 400°F (200°C) and bake the curry puffs for 25–30 minutes. Serve hot.

TURKEY AND POTATO TURNOVERS

SERVES

4 tbsp butter
1 large onion, sliced
1 large potato, peeled and
  thinly sliced
2 heaped cups roughly
  chopped turkey
¼ cup sour cream
2 sheets frozen puff pastry,
  thawed
milk, for brushing
salt and pepper

Melt the butter in a saucepan. Add the onion and cook until softened, then season really well, adding plenty of pepper. Add the potato and cook for 3–4 minutes longer. Transfer the onion and potato to a mixing bowl. Let cool, then mix in the turkey and sour cream.

Lay the pastry sheets on the work surface and cut out four rounds, using a small plate as a guide. Divide the filling among the pastry rounds. Brush the edges with milk, then fold over into half-moons and seal the edges well. Place on a baking sheet and chill for 30 minutes — preferably in the freezer.

Preheat the oven to 400°F (200°C) and bake the turnovers for 40 minutes. Serve hot.

PARTRIDGE PITHIVIERS WITH PORCINI AND RED WINE

MAKES

2 sheets frozen puff pastry, thawed

3 roast partridges

4 tbsp butter, plus extra for greasing

1 shallot, diced

4 oz (110 g) wild mushrooms

large handful of fresh chives, chopped

handful of chopped fresh parsley

milk, for glazing

salt and pepper

SAUCE

4 tbsp butter

2 shallots, sliced

2 oz (55 g) dried porcini, soaked in warm water for 30 minutes

1/2 cup port wine

1 cup red wine

1/2 cup stock

This is the classiest of pies. A pithiviers is shaped like a dome, with spiral marks on top. Roast the partridges in advance — they'll need about 15 minutes' cooking.

Lay the pastry sheets on the work surface and cut out 12 disks about the size of a coffee cup. Keep refrigerated.

Strip all the meat from the roasted partridges and shred it. Melt the butter in a saucepan, add the shallot and cook until softened. Add the mushrooms and cook for 1–2 minutes longer. Season to taste and mix in the partridge meat and herbs. Let cool.

To make the pies, place six of the pastry disks, evenly spaced, on a greased baking sheet. Pile up partridge filling in the center of each, leaving a border of pastry uncovered. Brush the border with milk and lay another pastry disk on top. Press down to give a little mound and seal the edges with a fork.

Use a blunt knife to score the pastry from the center top to the bottom in a semicircle, then repeat, working your way around each pithiviers to mark a wheel pattern. Brush the pastries with milk. Chill for at least 10 minutes or up to 24 hours.

When ready to cook, preheat the oven to 400°F (200°C) and bake the pithiviers until well browned, about 30 minutes.

Meanwhile, make the sauce. Melt the butter in a saucepan and cook the shallots until soft. Drain the mushrooms and add to the shallots. Season well and cook for 5 minutes. Add the port, bring to a boil and reduce by half. Add the wine and stock and bring back to a boil. Boil until thick and reduced to about ⅔ cup.

Spoon the sauce on serving plates and sit the fancy little pies on top.

PASTILLA

SERVES 🐔 🐔 🐔 🐔 🐔 🐔

4 confit duck legs (page 234),
   plus a little fat from the confit
1 onion, finely diced
1 cinnamon stick
handful of fresh parsley,
   cilantro and thyme, tied
   together, plus a handful of
   mixed parsley and cilantro,
   chopped
freshly ground black pepper
3 whole eggs, plus 2 yolks
2 tbsp confectioners' sugar
1 tsp ground cinnamon
handful of toasted almonds
7 oz (200 g) brik pastry or
   phyllo pastry
up to 4 tbsp butter, melted
a little vegetable oil (if using
   brik pastry)

Many people make Moroccan pastilla with squab, but I prefer it with duck. Brik, or brek, is the correct pastry to use. It can be bought from North African markets. I sometimes use phyllo pastry instead. If you do this, I advise you not to use too much butter on the layers or the pastilla will be greasy.

Heat the fat in a large cast-iron pan, add the onion and fry gently until translucent. Add the cinnamon stick and bundle of herbs, then the duck and give the pan a good shake. Grind in some pepper. Cover the duck with water, bring to a simmer and cook until warmed through, about 20 minutes. Using a slotted spoon, take all the bits out of the water and reserve the duck. Bring the liquid to a boil and reduce by half.

Beat the eggs and yolks together, then mix in three-quarters each of the confectioners' sugar and ground cinnamon. Pour this mixture into the water, off the heat, and stir vigorously until it thickens like custard. Grind the almonds, then add them to the custard and let cool.

Strip off the duck meat and shred it, discarding all skin and bones. Mix it with the chopped herbs. When the custard is cool, fold in the duck and herbs.

Preheat the oven to 400°F (200°C). Brush six little nonstick pie pans or blini pans with melted butter. Lay the pastry in the pans, leaving enough hanging over the edge so that it can be folded back to cover the filling. If you are using brik, use two or three layers of pastry and brush oil lightly between each one; for phyllo, use four layers with the minimum of melted butter.

Divide the filling among the pastry shells, then fold the pastry over and brush the tops with melted butter. Bake for 30 minutes. Let cool a little before unmolding. Sprinkle with the remaining confectioners' sugar and cinnamon, and serve.

WILD MUSHROOM TART
WITH PEPPERED GROUSE

SERVES

2 grouse
about 4 tbsp olive oil
large handful of fresh thyme
    sprigs
7 oz (200 g) mixed wild
    mushrooms
1 large shallot, diced
1 garlic clove, crushed
4 tbsp brandy
¼ cup mascarpone
4 individual baked pastry
    shells
large handful of chopped
    fresh parsley
salt and pepper

This little tart is rich yet homely. It could be served as a light lunch or the starting point of a hearty meal.

Preheat the oven to 400°F (200°C). Rub the grouse with oil and season well with salt and lots of black pepper. Stuff the cavities with thyme. Set an ovenproof frying pan over medium heat. When the pan is hot, add a little oil and then the grouse. Let them brown, turning three times to get an even color.

Transfer the pan to the oven and roast for 3 minutes. Give the pan a little shuffle, then roast for a few more minutes. At this point the grouse will be very pink at the center.

Meanwhile, clean and season the mushrooms. Remove the grouse to a plate and put the frying pan over medium heat. Add the shallot and garlic and cook until softened, about 5 minutes. Add the mushrooms and cook for 5 minutes longer.

Taste the mixture and season as necessary, then remove the mushrooms from the pan. Increase the heat, and when the pan is very hot add the brandy and flame it carefully. Drop the mushrooms back in the pan and add the mascarpone. Remove from the heat.

Warm the pastry shells in the oven for 5 minutes. Carve the meat from the grouse and slice it, then mix with some of the parsley and any juices from the birds. Pile the mushroom mixture in the hot pastry shells, top with the grouse and sprinkle with the last of the parsley. Serve immediately.

Budgets are a concern for many families, but budget does not have to mean cheap and nasty. I am inspired by the cuisines of Italy, China, Thailand and France, because they have great dishes in which the central ingredient is not a lump of meat but a staple such as flour, rice, couscous or lentils. This is truly clever cooking, where flavor is paramount.

The secret to doing these types of dishes well is to keep them simple. Add too many ingredients to a risotto and it will just be confused. Put too many fillings or sauces with pasta and the plate will never be clean (the sign of great food is a clean plate, after all). The greatest cooks have the confidence to make dishes simple; with just a few ingredients they can make something stunning.

Preparation is seriously important here. Don't rush and don't skimp. Buy good quality — it is not that expensive and what a difference it makes. Try to make your own stock too. Take time to nurture your dish — make it the most beautiful pot of rice or the best noodle dish in the world.

pasta, noodles and grains

SPAGHETTI WITH CURRIED CHICKEN BALLS

SERVES

1 large onion, finely chopped
4 tbsp vegetable oil
2 tbsp curry powder
4 tbsp milk
1²/₃ cups fresh bread crumbs
2¹/₄ lb (1 kg) ground chicken
handful of chopped fresh
   parsley, plus some other
   herbs if you like
1 lb (450 g) dried spaghetti
1¹/₄ cups heavy cream
salt and pepper

Put the onion, vegetable oil and curry powder in a large frying pan with a grind of pepper and some salt. Set over medium heat and slowly cook the onion until soft but not colored. Remove from the heat and lift out the onion, leaving the oil in the pan.

In a large bowl combine half the fried onion with the milk and bread crumbs. Add the ground chicken, lots of salt and pepper and the parsley. Mix really well until it becomes a paste rather than lumpy. Roll into balls a little smaller than a golf ball.

Put the frying pan over high heat and add the meatballs. Cook, turning, until they are well browned all over, about 10 minutes. Meanwhile, bring a big pot of salted water to a boil and cook the spaghetti according to the package directions.

When the meatballs are browned, add the rest of the fried onion and the cream and bring to a boil. Taste and season, if necessary. Cook for 5 minutes longer, then remove from the heat. Drain the spaghetti and add to the pan of meatballs and sauce. Mix gently together, then serve.

PENNE WITH RAGOUT OF GAME, SAUSAGE AND RED WINE

SERVES

1 large onion, sliced

4 tbsp butter

2 sprigs of fresh thyme

7 oz (200 g) spicy fresh pork sausage links, thickly sliced

8 pheasant legs or a mix of game pieces, about 2¼ lb (1 kg) in total

²/₃ cup all-purpose flour, seasoned with salt and pepper

3 tbsp olive oil

3 slices bacon, cut into strips

1 leek, chopped

4 tomatoes, chopped

1¼ cups stock

1¼ cups red wine

2 bay leaves

1½ lb (680 g) dried penne pasta

This is a great way to use up all the trimmings and bits of game that might be in the freezer.

Preheat the oven to 325°F (160°C). Melt the butter in an ovenproof casserole and sweat the onion gently with the thyme until soft but not colored. Add the spicy sausage and cook until crisp. Lift the sausages and onions from the pot and set aside.

Toss the pheasant, or whatever game you are using, in the seasoned flour. Add the oil to the pot, then fry the meat to give it a good color. Add the bacon, leek and tomatoes and fry with a bit of vigor, stirring to smash the tomatoes. Mix the remaining flour with the stock and red wine and pour into the casserole. Add the bay leaves, onion and sausages and bring to a boil. Cover and place in the oven to cook for 2 hours.

Take the pot from the oven and carefully lift out the game. Strip the meat from the bones and mince it with a chopping knife. Discard the game scraps and thyme sprigs. Stir the meat back into the ragout and keep warm.

Cook the pasta according to the package directions, then drain it and add to the ragout. Bring to a rapid boil, then serve.

ORECCHIETTE WITH PARTRIDGE

SERVES

4 partridge crowns (whole
  breasts on the bone)
4 tbsp butter
24 small button mushrooms
1 oz (30 g) dried porcini,
  crushed
1 cup chicken stock (page 20)
1¼ cups heavy cream
1 lb (450 g) orecchiette pasta
½ cup thick sour cream
large bunch of fresh chives,
  chopped
salt and pepper

Mushrooms, cream sauce and shredded partridge with soft pasta and loads of chives — fantastic.

Preheat the oven to 400°F (200°C). Rub the partridges with oil and seasoning, place in an ovenproof casserole and roast for 12 minutes. Remove from the oven and set the partridge aside.

Place the pot with all those lovely juices over medium heat. Add the butter, button mushrooms and porcini and cook for a few minutes. Pour in the stock, bring to a boil and reduce until the mixture is almost syrupy. Add the cream and bring to a boil, then season to taste. Meanwhile, shred the partridge meat and cook the pasta according to the package directions.

Stir the partridge and orecchiette into the mushroom mixture and bring to a boil once more. Spoon onto serving plates. Top each dish with a dollop of sour cream and sprinkle with chives.

FRESH PASTA

MAKES 1¼ LB (560 G)

4 cups "oo" pasta flour, plus
  extra for dusting
pinch of salt
4 whole eggs plus 3 egg yolks,
  beaten together
1 tbsp olive oil

"oo" flour is best for pasta. Softer flours absorb too much liquid so the pasta won't be strong enough.

Put the flour and salt in a food processor. Add half the beaten eggs and mix until incorporated. Add the oil and blend again. Add the remaining eggs a little at a time, feeling the texture of the mix regularly. When done it will be like large, loose bread crumbs that will come together as a dough if you squeeze them with your fingertips. You may not need to use all the egg, or you may need to add a little more.

Tip the mixture out onto a floured surface and push together, then knead until a dough forms. Wrap in plastic wrap and let rest for several hours before rolling and cutting as required.

BRAISED CANNELLONI

SERVES

olive oil
6 chicken thighs or legs
10 small shallots, chopped
10 plum or Roma tomatoes,
   chopped
²/₃ cup pitted black olives
10 pasta sheets 8–10 x
   6 inches (20–25 x 15 cm)
10 oz (285 g) large leaf spinach,
   stems removed
¹/₂ cup butter
freshly grated nutmeg
1 cup mascarpone
salt and pepper

Heat a little oil in an ovenproof casserole. Season the chicken, add to the pot and cook until well colored. Add the shallots and cook for a few more minutes. Add the tomatoes and olives and stir. Transfer to the oven to cook for 1 hour.

Let the chicken cool a little before stripping the meat from the bones. Using a slotted spoon, scoop out the solids from the sauce and mix with the chicken; you now have a thick mixture for filling the pasta and a thin sauce to cover the cannelloni.

Cook the pasta sheets, a few at a time, in a big pot of boiling salted water for 3 minutes if using freshly made pasta, or according to the package directions. Drain and rinse in cold water.

Meanwhile, in a large saucepan, cook the spinach in the butter, stirring constantly, until it has wilted. Season with nutmeg, salt and pepper. Let cool, then mix with the mascarpone and spread over the bottom of a baking dish.

Preheat the oven to 400°F (200°C). Spoon a generous amount of the chicken mixture along the middle of each pasta sheet and add a little more seasoning. Roll up and cut each roll into two cannelloni. Stack all the cannelloni on top of the spinach in the baking dish and pour the thin sauce over. Place in the oven and bake for 30 minutes. Drizzle some olive oil over and serve.

DUCK RAVIOLI

SERVES 🐔🐔🐔🐔🐔🐔

pasta dough (page 216)
1 egg, beaten
1 fresh red chili, sliced
2 green onions, chopped
small bunch of cilantro leaves

FILLING
2¹/₄ lb (1 kg) duck legs
olive oil
2 carrots, chopped
1 onion, chopped
1 celery stalk, chopped
2 oz (55 g) galangal, chopped
1 garlic clove, crushed
1 star anise
4 tbsp port wine
1 cup red wine
2 cups chicken stock (page 20)
4 tbsp dark soy sauce
4 tbsp fish sauce
salt and pepper

BROTH
1 duck carcass or bones left
  over from a roast duck
2 tbsp fish sauce
2 oz (55 g) fresh ginger, sliced
1 lemongrass stalk, peeled and
  chopped
2 star anise
small handful of cilantro
  (coriander) roots, chopped
1 tbsp dark soy sauce
¹/₂ tsp toasted sesame oil

This is a very complex dish but rewarding to make.

Preheat the oven to 375°F (190°C). To make the filling, trim any excess fat from the duck legs and season well. Heat a little oil in a frying pan, add the duck and fry until well browned on all sides.

Heat some more oil in an ovenproof casserole and soften the vegetables with the galangal, garlic and star anise. Add the port and red wine and boil until reduced to a glaze. Add the duck legs and stock and bring to a boil, skimming. Add the soy and fish sauces, then transfer to the oven. Cook until the duck is very tender, about 1 hour.

Meanwhile, make the duck broth. Put all the ingredients in a pot with 2 quarts (8 cups) water, bring to a boil, and simmer for about 1 hour.

Roll the pasta dough through a pasta machine following the manufacturer's instructions. Cut the dough into 12 disks about 4 inches (10 cm) in diameter. Keep them covered with plastic wrap until you are ready to fill them.

Take the casserole from the oven and remove the duck legs. Strain the liquid, put it back in the pot and bring to a boil. Keep bubbling until you have a thick sauce. Meanwhile, shred the meat from the duck legs, then mix it with the sauce.

Place a spoonful of duck in the center of half of the pasta disks. Brush the edges with beaten egg and press the remaining disks on top. Pinch around the edges to seal well.

Bring a large pot of salted water to a boil and add a dash of oil. Working in two batches, cook the ravioli for about 4 minutes (they will be done 2 minutes after they float to the surface).

Meanwhile, strain the duck broth into a warmed serving bowl. As the ravioli cook, put them into the broth. Serve garnished with chili, green onions and cilantro.

CHICKEN LAKSA

SERVES

8 oz (225 g) thick noodles
8 oz (225 g) fish balls
vegetable oil
8 oz (225 g) large raw shrimp
1 cup canned coconut milk
5 cups chicken stock
1 tsp fish sauce
2 cups cubed chicken breast
²/₃ cup shredded choy sum
¹/₂ cup bean sprouts
¹/₄ cup cucumber in fine strips
bunch of cilantro, chopped
a little hot chili powder

LAKSA PASTE
¹/₂ tsp coriander seeds
pinch of cumin seeds
1 onion, chopped
¹/₄ cup chopped fresh ginger
5 cilantro (coriander) roots
1 lemongrass stalk, peeled
  and chopped
4 Kaffir lime leaves, chopped
¹/₃ cup candlenuts or blanched
  almonds
1 tsp shrimp paste
4 garlic cloves
1 tsp ground turmeric
1 tsp ground coriander
2 tsp ground cumin
2 large red (serrano) chilies,
  deseeded and chopped
6 tbsp red curry paste

Buy laksa paste in a jar if you don't want to make your own. Indonesian markets also sell prepared fish balls, plus *sambal oelek* to serve on the side.

Cook the noodles following the package directions, then drain and keep in a warm place. Meanwhile, fry the fish balls on all sides in a little oil; set aside. Peel and devein the shrimp.

To make the laksa paste, toast the coriander and cumin seeds in a dry pan until they release their aromas and color slightly. Combine in a food processor with the onion, ginger, cilantro roots, lemongrass, lime leaves, nuts, shrimp paste, garlic and 4 teaspoons vegetable oil, and puree.

Heat ½ cup oil in a large pan and add the turmeric, ground coriander and cumin, and the chilies. Fry, stirring all the time, until fragrant, about 5 minutes. Add the spice paste to the pan and cook, stirring, until you have a very aromatic jamlike paste, 5–8 minutes. When done, set aside.

Meanwhile, heat a little oil in a wok and fry the red curry paste until it darkens, about 10 minutes. Add the laksa paste and let them bubble together until dark and aromatic. Add the coconut milk, chicken stock and fish sauce and bring to a boil. Add the shrimp, chicken and fish balls and cook for 5 minutes.

Pour the chicken laksa into big serving bowls and add the noodles. Garnish with the choy sum, bean sprouts and cucumber. Sprinkle with chopped cilantro and a little chili powder. Serve *sambal oelek* separately in a small bowl for people to help themselves. If they are your friends, warn them if you've chosen a blow-your-head-off type!

PHAT THAI

SERVES

1¼ lb (560 g) dried thick, flat
   rice noodles (*banh pho*)
3 skinless, boneless chicken
   breast halves
½ cup vegetable oil
¾ cup finely chopped garlic
bunch of cilantro, roots
   separated (coriander root)
   and leaves picked from stems
20 medium raw shrimp, peeled
   and deveined
1 cup chopped pickled turnip
2½ tbsp sugar
4 eggs, beaten
4 tbsp fish sauce
1½ tbsp oyster sauce
6 cups bean sprouts
bunch of green onions, cut
   diagonally
⅔ cup crushed roasted
   peanuts
3 fresh red chilies, deseeded
   and minced
1 lime, quartered

Phat Thai (pronounced pad Thai) is central Thailand's greatest snack food, sold at street markets within Bangkok and the many towns that surround it. Phat Thai is never very spicy; the chilies are added at the end, usually by the consumer. For me the special ingredient is pickled turnip, which gives the sour dimension and crunchy texture that makes the best phat Thai. Add the lime juice at the last minute — if it cooks it becomes bitter.

Soak the rice noodles in cold water for up to 2 hours, then drain and keep to one side. Cut the chicken into long, thin strips slightly thicker than the noodles.

In a wok, heat the oil over high heat. When shimmering, add the garlic and cilantro roots and stir for a few moments. Add the chicken, shrimp and pickled turnip and cook for 30 seconds. Add the sugar and then the eggs and cook for 30 seconds longer. Stir in the fish sauce and oyster sauce. Add the noodles and toss for about 2 minutes.

Add the bean sprouts and green onions and toss well. Put the noodles in a serving dish and finish with cilantro leaves, roasted peanuts, chilies and wedges of lime.

TURKEY SOUP NOODLES WITH WATER CHESTNUTS

SERVES

2 oz (55 g) fresh ginger, peeled
2 oz (55 g) garlic cloves, peeled (about ½ cup)
2 oz (55 g) cilantro (coriander) roots, plus leaves from a few cilantro sprigs
14 oz (400 g) turkey cutlets
vegetable oil
1 lb 5 oz (600 g) thick Chinese wheat noodles, or udon
1 cup sugar snap peas
8 oz (225 g) can water chestnuts, drained and sliced
4 tbsp soy sauce
½ cup *kecap manis*
⅔ cup Thai fish sauce
6 cups chicken stock (page 20)
1 cup bean sprouts
salt and pepper

Pound the ginger, garlic and cilantro roots together to make a paste and set aside.

Heat a ridged cast-iron grill pan until very hot. Rub the turkey cutlets with oil and season with salt and pepper. Pan-grill on both sides until cooked through. Cut the turkey into fine strips and keep warm.

Heat some oil in a hot wok. When it is shimmering, add the ginger paste and stir until fragrant. Add the noodles and stir-fry for about 2 minutes. Add the sugar snap peas and the water chestnuts. Toss well and cook for 1 more minute. Add the soy sauce, *kecap manis* and fish sauce and cook for 2 minutes longer. Pour in the stock and bring to a boil.

Ladle the soup noodles into serving bowls. Top with the turkey, bean sprouts and cilantro leaves and serve.

CHICKEN AND SAKE NOODLES WITH EGG AND GREEN ONIONS

SERVES

3 boneless chicken breast
  halves

7 oz (200 g) green onions

4 tbsp vegetable oil

4 oz (110 g) fresh ginger,
  cut into very fine strips
  (about 1/2 cup)

2 oz (55 g) garlic cloves (about
  1/2 cup), sliced paper-thin

1 1/4 lb (560 g) precooked udon
  noodles

1 3/4 cups sake

3 eggs, beaten

4 tbsp soy sauce

This is quick and delicious. Udon noodles are the fat, soft, white ones from Japan. If yours don't come precooked (known in the UK as straight-to-wok), they'll probably need cooking or soaking first.

Cut the chicken breasts into strips about 3/4 inch (2 cm) wide and the full length of the breast. Set aside. Cut the green onions into pieces the width of your thumb, keeping the white and green parts separate.

Heat a wok and add the oil. Once the oil is hot, add the chicken followed by the ginger and garlic and stir-fry until the chicken is just colored, about 2 minutes. Add the white parts of the green onions and stir-fry briefly before adding the noodles and the green parts of the green onions. Toss for a couple of minutes so the noodles heat through.

Pour in the sake, which should boil right away. Stir, then add the beaten eggs. Add the soy sauce and stir well. When the egg is just starting to cook, remove the wok from the heat and stir so the egg finishes cooking in the residual heat.

DUCK SOUP NOODLES WITH SCALLOPS AND GINGER

SERVES

BROTH

1 Chinese roast duck (page 174)
1/2 tbsp Szechuan peppercorns
2 tbsp sliced fresh ginger
1/2 oz (15 g) star anise
2 green onions
1/3 oz (10 g) cinnamon sticks
   (about 6)
1 cup soy sauce
2/3 cup Shaoxing wine
2/3 cup yellow rock sugar
4 tbsp toasted sesame oil
2 tbsp sliced garlic cloves

GARNISH

2 1/4 lb (1 kg) wonton noodles
1 lb (450 g) sea scallops
7 oz (200 g) fresh ginger,
   peeled and cut into
   matchsticks
7 oz (200 g) green onions,
   sliced diagonally
5 oz (140 g) pea or snow pea
   shoots

Strip the meat from the duck and set aside. Chop the carcass into four or five pieces. Put the carcass in a pot, cover with about 4 quarts (16 cups) water and bring to a boil. Simmer for 10 minutes, skimming as necessary, then reduce the heat to a low simmer. Add all the remaining broth ingredients and continue simmering for 1 hour.

Meanwhile, bring a pot of water to a boil, add the wonton noodles and cook according to the package directions. Drain and keep the noodles warm by covering them with plastic wrap. Slice or shred the duck meat, discarding all skin.

When the broth is ready, strain it into a clean pan and adjust the seasoning to taste.

Cut the scallops crosswise into thin slices. Put a heavy frying pan over high heat and sear them for 30 seconds on each side.

Divide the noodles, scallops and sliced duck among serving bowls. Ladle in the broth and scatter the ginger, green onions and pea shoots on top before serving.

PAN-GRILLED PARTRIDGE WITH BLACK CABBAGE AND POLENTA

SERVES

1 large onion, sliced
¹/₂ cup butter
12 oz (340 g) cavolo nero
  (Tuscan black cabbage)
1¹/₂ cups cremini mushrooms
²/₃ oz (20 g) Parmesan, shaved
4 tbsp olive oil
12 partridge breasts
6 branches of fresh rosemary
delicious extra-virgin olive oil
salt and pepper

POLENTA
1¹/₄ cups milk
1 garlic clove, crushed
²/₃ cup polenta
¹/₂ cup heavy cream
3 tbsp freshly grated Parmesan
  cheese
¹/₃ cup mascarpone

Char the breasts well so they are slightly bitter and provide a real contrast to the sweet, salty polenta and spicy cabbage. You can also serve this as a first course.

Start with the polenta. Put 1 cup water in a saucepan with the milk, garlic and some salt and pepper and bring to a rolling boil. Add the polenta, stirring constantly in a clockwise direction, and keep stirring until the mixture thickens and comes back to a boil. Reduce the heat to very low and cook, stirring very frequently, for 45 minutes. Add the cream and Parmesan cheese and continue cooking over low heat for 10 minutes. Remove the pan from the heat and stir in the mascarpone. Keep warm.

While the polenta is cooking, preheat the oven to 350°F (175°C). In a heavy frying pan, fry the onion gently in the butter until softened. Meanwhile, strip the leaves from the stems of the cavolo nero and cook the leaves for 10 minutes in boiling salted water; drain. Add the mushrooms to the onion and season well, then add the cavolo nero leaves and cook gently for 15 minutes.

Put a ridged cast-iron grill pan over high heat to get really hot. Meanwhile, spoon the polenta onto heatproof serving plates, top with the mushroom mixture and scatter the Parmesan shavings over. Keep warm in the oven while you cook the partridges.

Oil and season the partridge breasts, then lay them skin-side down in the grill pan. Place the rosemary on top. Cook for 3 minutes, then turn over and place the rosemary back on top. Transfer the pan to the oven to finish cooking for 5 minutes.

Serve the partridge with the polenta and vegetables, drizzled with your fabulous olive oil.

CHICKEN BIRYANI

SERVES

1³/4 cups basmati rice
2 tbsp butter
1 large onion, finely sliced
1 bay leaf
3 cardamom pods
1 small cinnamon stick
1 tsp ground turmeric
4 skinless, boneless chicken
   breast halves, cut into large
   chunks
6 tbsp hot Indian-style curry
   paste
handful of raisins
4 cups chicken stock (page 20)
large handful of toasted
   sliced almonds
large handful of chopped
   cilantro

Rinse the rice well, then set aside to drain. Heat the butter in a saucepan and cook the onion with the bay leaf, cardamom and cinnamon for 10 minutes. Sprinkle in the turmeric, then add the chicken and curry paste and cook, stirring, until aromatic.

Add the rice and raisins and continue cooking and stirring for a few minutes. When fragrant, add the stock and bring to a boil. Cover with a tight-fitting lid. When it starts to boil vigorously, reduce the heat and cook for 10 minutes.

Remove from the heat but don't lift the lid off the pan. Let the biryani sit for 20 minutes. Just before serving, stir in half the almonds and cilantro, then serve with the rest of the almonds and cilantro scattered over the top.

CHICKEN AND WILD ONION RISOTTO

SERVES

1 tbsp butter, plus 3 tbsp for
   finishing
1 tbsp olive oil
4 shallots, diced
4 garlic cloves, crushed
10 oz (285 g) skinless,
   boneless chicken thighs,
   cut into chunks
2 cups arborio rice
about 4 cups boiling chicken
   stock (page 20)
1 cup freshly grated Parmesan
   cheese
large handful of ramp (wild
   onion) leaves, torn

When making a risotto it is important that the stock and rice are at a similar temperature, so that the heat doesn't fall when you add the stock. If it does, the rice may not cook properly.

Ramp (wild onion) can be found in specialty vegetable markets and farmers' markets in the spring. Be careful as it is a lot stronger than it looks. If you can't get ramp, try a mix of soft herbs such as sage, basil, chives and chervil.

Heat 1 tablespoon butter and the oil in a large, heavy pan. Add the shallots and cook until just translucent, then add two of the garlic cloves and the chicken and cook for 3—4 minutes longer. Add the rice and stir for a couple of minutes to coat the grains.

Add a couple of ladles of boiling stock to the rice and stir with a wooden spatula until all the liquid has been absorbed and the rice can be scraped from the bottom of the pan. Keep adding ladles of stock, stirring and scraping all the time to prevent sticking. After 15–20 minutes the rice grains will be tender but still firm to the bite and the risotto mixture will be creamy and moist. You may not need to add all of the stock.

Add the Parmesan and remaining butter and whip with a wooden spoon to put more air into the risotto. Throw in the ramp leaves and serve immediately.

CHICKEN PAELLA

SERVES 🐔🐔🐔🐔🐔🐔

½ cup olive oil
2 white onions, diced
4 garlic cloves, crushed
4 overripe tomatoes, chopped
4 oz (110 g) Spanish chorizo
    links, sliced
1 fresh red chili, chopped
30 saffron strands
2 heaped cups Spanish
    paella rice
5 cups vegetable stock
1 red onion, diced
7 oz (200 g) fresh mussels
½ cup white wine
10 oz (285 g) peeled large raw
    shrimp, deveined
10 oz (285 g) skinless chicken
    breast halves, cut into pieces
4 oz (110 g) green beans
1 tsp smoked paprika
large handful of cilantro leaves
salt and pepper

Nearly every traveler to Spain has experienced a paella — some good, some not so good, depending on the freshness of the ingredients, the care taken with the seasoning and the speed at which it is served. The quality of the rice is important. Look for a package with grains that are whole, with none broken.

Heat a paella pan (or large wok). Add half of the olive oil and then the white onions. Cook gently for 3–4 minutes. Add the garlic and cook for 1 minute, then add the tomatoes, chorizo and chili. Increase the heat and add 20 saffron strands followed by the rice. Cook for 3–4 minutes. Pour in the stock and bring to a boil. Reduce the heat to a simmer and let cook, stirring occasionally so it doesn't stick and burn.

Meanwhile, heat the remaining oil in a large pot over very high heat. Add the red onion and fry for 2 minutes, then throw in the mussels. Pour the wine over the top, stir well and let cook for 5 minutes, stirring occasionally.

Add the shrimp and chicken, followed by the beans, smoked paprika and remaining saffron. Stir, then place a tight-fitting lid on top. Cook until the shrimp are pink and all the mussels are open (discard any that don't open), about 3 minutes.

By now the rice should be cooked, so add half the chicken-seafood mixture to it and stir. Add the cilantro to the remaining chicken-seafood mixture and spoon it into the middle of the paella. Take the pan to the table, open a good bottle of rioja and share with your friends.

If you can master a few great dishes and think it is time to become a really great cook, learn the art of preserving. Confit, terrines, sausages, pastrami — all are foods that have traditionally been put aside for winter when there is little in the way of fresh produce.

A great cook utilizes everything and does not buy a chicken breast in a pack, but buys a whole bird and debones it. The legs of that bird cooked and stored in fat, as the recipes here show, are something of a miracle — soft, juicy and sweet.

The first time you make pâté it may seem a chore, but do persist. Make it a few times and you will get used to it and see how simple it really is. The game terrine is the most difficult and time-consuming recipe here, but you will enjoy the flavor. Never again will you go to the deli and ask for a slice of their stuff.

I love pastrami and want more people to make it so the whole world can eat it. Turkey pastrami takes a few days, but so what? Start Thursday and by Sunday lunch people will be eating pastrami with bagels and pickles, their mouths agape that you — yes, you! — made it. The bonus is that these treats will keep in your refrigerator for a week or more.

confit, terrines, pâtés and pastrami

CONFIT DUCK

SERVES

6 cumin seeds
12 coriander seeds
3 juniper berries
1 garlic clove, sliced, plus
   1 whole head garlic, halved
   horizontally
$^2/_3$ cup sea salt
6 duck legs
small bunch of fresh thyme
1 branch of fresh rosemary
about 2 cups duck or goose fat
2 bay leaves
1 tsp black peppercorns

The fat used to make the confit can be reused over and over, the flavors improving every time.

The day before cooking, put the cumin and coriander seeds in a dry pan and toast until they are slightly colored and aromatic. Remove to a board and crush them with the flat side of a knife blade. Crush the juniper berries and sliced garlic as well and mix the spices with the salt. Rub this mixture over the duck. Scatter the thyme, rosemary and halved garlic over the duck and leave in a cool place for 24 hours, turning them two or three times.

Next day, pat the duck dry with paper towels, but don't rinse off the marinade. (The salt extracts the water from the meat cells, which will be reinflated with fat as the duck cooks gently. If you rinse it, you will simply reinflate the cells with water.)

Put the duck in a cast-iron casserole and cover with the duck or goose fat. Add the bay leaves and peppercorns. If you have the time to keep an eye on the oven, I find that slowly raising the temperature to a peak and then reducing it steadily helps to keep those cells filled with fat. I start at 300°F (150°C) and raise the temperature a bit every 15 minutes for 45 minutes until it reaches 350°F (175°C), then reduce at the same rate for 45 minutes longer. Otherwise, cook at 325°F (160°C) for 1½ hours. At this point the meat should almost be falling off the bone.

You can store the confit duck very simply by placing it in a bowl, covering it with the fat and keeping it in the refrigerator. As long as it stays covered with fat it will keep for weeks.

CONFIT DUCK WITH WHITE BEANS, SAUSAGE AND PANCETTA

SERVES

2 cups dried white beans,
soaked overnight in cold
water
1 carrot, chopped
1 onion, chopped
4 tomatoes, chopped
1 bouquet garni
2 sprigs of fresh flat-leaf
parsley
2 sprigs of fresh sage, plus
extra sage leaves for garnish
4 tbsp olive oil
4 oz (110 g) pancetta, cut into
thin strips
7 oz (200 g) Toulouse sausage
links, cooked and sliced
4–6 confit duck legs (page 234)

If you want to cheat, you can use prepared confit duck, which can be bought in jars or crocks from supermarkets and specialty food stores.

Drain and rinse the soaked beans, then put them in a large pot and cover with cold water. Add the vegetables, herbs, olive oil and pancetta and bring to a boil. Simmer until the beans are soft, about 1 hour. Drain off the excess liquid and discard the bouquet garni and herb sprigs. The beans should have the texture of a thick soup. Add the sliced sausage and heat through.

While the beans are cooking, preheat the oven to 350°F (175°C). Remove the confit duck legs from their fat. Set an ovenproof frying pan on high heat. When it is hot, add the duck legs skin-side down and cook for 4 minutes. Turn the legs over and transfer the pan to the oven. Cook for about 20 minutes.

Pour the bean mixture into shallow bowls and sit a piece of duck on top of each. Garnish with sage leaves.

CONFIT CHICKEN WITH MASH AND GREEN SAUCE

SERVES

2 cardamom pods

12 coriander seeds

3 juniper berries

²/₃ cup sea salt

small bunch of fresh thyme,
  leaves picked from stems

1 whole head garlic, halved
  horizontally, plus 1 garlic
  clove, crushed

6 chicken legs

about 2 cups duck or goose fat

pared zest of 1 orange

pared zest of 1 lemon

2 bay leaves

small bunch of fresh rosemary

1 tsp black peppercorns

mashed potatoes (page 157)
  and salsa verde (page 66),
  for serving

Tip: confit rabbit legs are absolutely delicious and only need a slightly longer cooking time than chicken. You can confit pheasant legs too, in which case follow the cooking times for confit duck — pheasant has a more fibrous musculature than chicken and the meat will take longer to reach tenderness.

This is all about soft, moist chicken legs served with great buttery mash and a tart but herby rich sauce.

The day before cooking, put the cardamom pods and coriander seeds in a dry pan and toast until they are slightly colored and aromatic. Remove to a board and crush them with the flat side of a knife blade. Crush the juniper berries as well and mix the spices with the salt, thyme and crushed clove of garlic. Rub the mixture over the chicken, then leave in a cool place for 24 hours, turning the legs two or three times.

Next day, preheat the oven to 300°F (150°C). Pat the chicken dry with paper towels, but don't rinse off the marinade. Put the chicken in a cast-iron casserole and cover with the duck or goose fat. Add the halved garlic head, orange and lemon zest, bay leaves, rosemary and peppercorns and place in the oven. Cook for 10 minutes. Increase the heat to 350°F (175°C) and cook for 15 minutes, then turn the temperature up to 400°F (200°C). After another 15 minutes, turn up to 450°F (230°C) and cook for about 10 minutes. The fat should be bubbling. Now, start to reduce the heat: 400°F (200°C) for 15 minutes, then 350°F (175°C) for another 15 minutes. Turn off the oven and leave the chicken inside for 10 minutes or so longer. At this point the meat should almost be falling off the bone.

Alternatively, cook at 325°F (160°C) for 1 hour. Serve with mashed potatoes and salsa verde.

CHICKEN LIVER PÂTÉ

SERVES

1 lb (450 g) chicken livers
1¼ cups soft butter
14 oz (400 g) slab bacon, diced
3 onions, diced
2 tbsp brandy
freshly grated nutmeg
clarified butter, to cover
  (optional)
salt and pepper

This pâté is so simple to make, although few people will ever think it. Give it a try and you'll be hooked.

Check the chicken livers for any greenish stains and cut them off, because even a scrap will make the pâté bitter. At the same time, pull each lobe away from its connecting threads.

Heat one-third of the butter in a nonstick frying pan until just foaming. Add the bacon and onions, season well and cook until the onions are soft, 8–10 minutes. Add the livers and fry quickly until cooked but still quite soft in the middle, about 2 minutes.

Increase the heat. Add the brandy and carefully ignite it with a match, tilting the pan to spread the flames across the livers. Add a little salt, pepper and grated nutmeg. Remove from the heat.

Transfer the mixture to a food processor and blend. For an extra-smooth finish, press the pâté through a coarse sieve. Return the pâté to the food processor and blend in the remaining butter. Check the seasoning, then press the pâté into a ceramic crock or individual pots and chill well.

The surface of the pâté will gradually oxidize — that is, it will darken in contact with the air. This doesn't affect the flavor, but if you wish to avoid this, cover the pâté with a thin layer of clarified butter once it's in the pot(s).

DUCK LIVER TERRINE

SERVES

1 lb (450 g) butter
vegetable oil
1 onion, finely chopped
3 garlic cloves, minced
6 black peppercorns
6 bay leaves
6 sprigs of fresh thyme
1¼ cups dry white wine
1 lb 5 oz (600 g) duck livers,
    any green bits removed
7 oz (200 g) duck foie gras,
    chopped
2 eggs
2 tbsp Madeira
2 tbsp port wine
2 tbsp cognac
freshly grated nutmeg
salt and pepper

Line the bottom of a 2 lb (900 g) terrine mold (I use a Le Creuset terrine) with parchment paper. Heat a little of the butter and some oil in a frying pan and cook the onion and garlic until soft, without coloring. Add the peppercorns, bay leaves, thyme and white wine. Bring to a boil and let reduce to a syrup.

Put the duck livers, foie gras and eggs in a food processor and blend to a paste. Push the paste through a very fine sieve into a large mixing bowl.

Melt the remaining butter in a saucepan. In a separate small pan, boil the Madeira, port and cognac until reduced by half, then add to the hot butter. Strain the onion and wine mixture into the butter as well, pressing down to extract all the flavors, then discard the solids. Stir the boozy butter and liver mixtures together until combined. Season with nutmeg, salt and pepper.

Preheat the oven to 300°F (150°C). Pour the mix into the lined terrine mold. Lay a dish towel on the bottom of a roasting pan and set the mold on top. Pour 2 cups water into the pan around the mold. Cover with a lid or foil and place in the oven. Cook for 25–30 minutes. Remove from the oven and let cool for a few hours before unmolding.

DUCK RILLETTES

SERVES

1 tbsp sea salt
1 lb (450 g) duck legs
10 garlic cloves, chopped
3 sprigs of fresh thyme, leaves
   picked from stems
1 lb (450 g) fresh pork belly
   (side pork), cut into strips
2–4 cups goose or duck fat
1 tsp ground black pepper
salt

The day before cooking, rub half the sea salt into the duck legs, then layer in a container with half the garlic and thyme. Do the same with the pork. Cover and refrigerate overnight.

Next day, preheat the oven to 325°F (160°C). Remove the meat from the refrigerator and rub off the salt, garlic and thyme. Place in an ovenproof casserole and cover with goose or duck fat. Bring to a boil, then transfer to the oven to cook for 2 hours.

Drain the meat, reserving the fat. When it is cool enough to handle, but still warm, flake the pork and keep to one side. Do the same with the duck, making sure there are no bones. Shred the skin finely.

Mix the pork and duck together well and add the pepper and salt to taste. Gradually add about two-thirds of the goose or duck fat, mixing well, until the rillettes is the consistency of mayonnaise.

Check the seasoning (it needs to be well seasoned), then pack into little pots and cover with the remaining fat. Chill until set.

GAME TERRINE

SERVES

6 squab breasts

14 oz (400 g) *lardo* (cured Italian lard)

1¼ lb (560 g) skinless, boneless chicken

2¼ lb (1 kg) duck or chicken livers, or a mix

8 oz (225 g) duck breasts

4 oz (110 g) boneless partridge or pheasant, or a mix

1 tbsp chopped garlic

1 tbsp ground allspice

1 tbsp chopped fresh parsley

3 tbsp Armagnac

1½ cups dry white wine

1 cup concentrated stock

onions Madagascar, for serving (page 246)

salt and pepper

This is more opulent than most other terrines. Don't skip the marinating process or the result will be dry and have little flavor. Note that you need kitchen scales to make this successfully, although you can approximate the weights if necessary.

Two days before serving, cut all the meat into ½-inch (1.2 cm) pieces, putting all the best pieces to one side. If the squab breasts are quite small, leave them whole. From the best bits, weigh out 6 oz (170 g) *lardo*, 9 oz (255 g) chicken, 1 lb (450 g) livers and 3 oz (85 g) duck. Set these aside with all the squab and partridge or pheasant.

Grind all the remaining meat and fat, then add the garlic and half each of the allspice, parsley, Armagnac and wine. Season the chopped meat and sprinkle with the remaining allspice, parsley, Armagnac and wine. Refrigerate both mixes overnight.

Next day, preheat the oven to 350°F (175°C). Combine the ground meat mixture and concentrated stock, then stir in the chopped meat. Press into a well-greased 2 lb (900 g) terrine mold, packing down well. Cover tightly with parchment paper and then foil.

Lay a dish towel on the bottom of a roasting pan and set the mold in it. Pour warm water into the pan to surround the mold. Place in the oven and reduce the heat to 325°F (160°C). Cook for 1¼ hours. Remove the terrine from the oven and let cool in the pan of water for 1 hour.

Take the mold from the water and weigh the contents down with something like a big book. Set on a tray and refrigerate overnight. Keep the juices that leak out; they will be gelatinous and can be chopped and served alongside the terrine.

Next day, unmold the terrine and slice it for serving.

ONIONS MADAGASCAR

SERVES

2 tsp olive oil
1 lb (450 g) small, round
   shallots
5 tbsp vinegar
1 tsp sugar
6 tbsp tomato paste
6 tbsp raisins
1 bay leaf
2 sprigs of fresh thyme
handful of chopped fresh
   parsley

If you can't find shallots, boiling onions (onions picked when young and small) will work just as nicely here. The acid in the pickle cuts through the fat of a terrine perfectly.

Heat the oil in a saucepan and sauté the shallots until they are just colored. Add the vinegar and sugar and cook until brown, then add the tomato paste and raisins.

Add all the herbs and ½ cup water. Partially cover the saucepan and simmer very gently until the shallots are soft, 35–40 minutes. The longer and slower the cooking, the more intense the flavor will be, and if you leave them in the refrigerator for a day before serving, the flavor will improve further.

Also good with onions Madagascar: rillettes 🐓 pâtés 🐓 smoked fish 🐓 salads made with confit chicken 🐓 buffet foods

SMOKED DUCK SALAD WITH ORANGE AND FENNEL

SERVES 🐔🐔🐔🐔🐔🐔🐔🐔

½ cup packed brown sugar
1 cup Lapsang souchong tea
  leaves
handful of couscous or rice
4 duck breasts
salt and pepper

SALAD
1 large fennel bulb
½ lemon
2 oranges, peeled and sliced
4 tbsp olive oil
small bunch of fresh dill,
  leaves picked from stems

You can buy smoked duck — and smoked chicken — but here is a quick and effective means of smoking at home. The salad is worth serving on its own, too. Once smoked, duck breasts will last about a week.

Line a wok with a sheet of foil. Mix together the brown sugar, tea leaves and couscous or rice and spread evenly around the bottom of the wok. Set a rack in the wok. Score the duck skin and season with salt, then place the duck skin-side up on the rack. Cover with a tight-fitting lid.

Turn the heat under the wok to high. After about 10 minutes it will start to smoke. Leave the wok on the heat for 15 minutes longer, then remove from the heat and let smoke, still covered, for 15 more minutes.

Transfer the smoked duck skin-side down to a cold frying pan and place over high heat. Leave it for 6–7 minutes, so the fat melts slowly and the skin becomes crisp. Turn the duck breasts over and remove the pan from the heat. The skin should be crisp, the flesh lean. The flavor of smoke should run all the way through the meat. Let cool.

To make the salad, shave the fennel, sprinkle with salt and squeeze the lemon juice over. Add the oranges and olive oil, but don't stir in the dill until just before serving.

Slice the duck very thinly lengthwise, spread it out on serving plates and scatter the salad over.

TURKEY PASTRAMI

MAKES 1¾ LB (800 G)

2 oz (55 g) black peppercorns
  (about ⅓ cup), plus 1 tbsp
large handful of crushed
  juniper berries
2 tbsp coriander seeds, crushed
1 cup packed brown sugar
1 heaped cup sea salt
6 garlic cloves, crushed
2 tsp fresh thyme leaves
1 tsp whole cloves
3 bay leaves
2 small turkey breast halves,
  14 oz (400 g) each

SMOKE

½ cup packed brown sugar
1 cup Lapsang souchong tea
  leaves
handful of couscous or rice

Variation: you can smoke the pastrami in the barbecue instead. Combine 10 oz (285 g) green wood chips, 3 cups tea leaves and two handfuls of rice. Place the mixture on a sheet of foil and lay it over the glowing coals. Cover and smoke as above.

This takes a few days to make, but is delicious.

Grind 2 oz (55 g) peppercorns in a small food processor or blender until they are crushed, then tip them into a fine sieve and shake gently. You need to sieve the crushed peppercorns twice: the kibble that is left over is for the pastrami. Combine the kibble, juniper and coriander seeds and set aside.

In a saucepan combine 2 cups water with the brown sugar and salt. Bring to a boil, stirring until the salt and sugar have dissolved. Remove from the heat and stir in 1 tablespoon whole black peppercorns, plus the garlic, thyme, cloves and bay leaves. Let this brine cool.

Place the turkey breasts in a big plastic container and pour the cooled brine over them, making sure the turkey is completely covered. Refrigerate for 48 hours.

To smoke, line a wok with a sheet of foil. Mix together the brown sugar, tea leaves and couscous or rice and spread evenly around the bottom of the work. Set a wire rack on top.

Remove the turkey from the brine, rinse under cold water and pat dry with paper towels. Cover the turkey with the pepper and juniper rub, pressing it into the surface. Lay the turkey skin-side down on the rack, then cover and smoke until it is cooked all the way through, about 2 hours. Remove from the smoker and let cool. The turkey will continue to gain flavor the longer you let it rest — wrap it tightly in plastic wrap and refrigerate up to 1 week.

Slice the turkey and serve with pickles, mustard, mayo, Belgian endive and sliced soft bread.

DUCK PASTRAMI WITH MUSTARD SAUCE

SERVES 🐔🐔🐔🐔🐔🐔🐔🐔🐔🐔🐔🐔

1 cup packed brown sugar
1 heaped cup sea salt
1 tbsp black peppercorns
6 garlic cloves, crushed
2 tsp fresh thyme leaves
1 tsp whole cloves
3 bay leaves
1³/₄ lb (800 g) duck breasts
large handful of crushed
  juniper berries
2 tbsp coriander seeds, crushed

SMOKE
¹/₂ cup packed brown sugar
1 cup Lapsang souchong tea
  leaves
handful of couscous or rice

MUSTARD SAUCE
1¹/₄ cups heavy cream
1¹/₄ cups Dijon mustard

In a saucepan combine 2 cups water with the brown sugar and salt. Bring to a boil, stirring until the salt and sugar have dissolved. Remove from the heat and stir in the peppercorns, garlic, thyme, cloves and bay leaves. Let this brine cool.

Place the duck breasts in a big plastic container and pour the cooled brine over them, making sure the duck is completely immersed. Chill for 24 hours.

To smoke, line a wok with a sheet of foil. Mix together the brown sugar, tea leaves and couscous or rice and spread evenly around the bottom of the work. Set a wire rack on top.

Remove the duck from the brine, rinse under cold water and pat dry with paper towels. Mix together the juniper and coriander and rub all over the duck, pressing it into the surface.

Lay the duck skin-side down on the rack. Cover and smoke until it has cooked all the way through, about 30 minutes. Remove from the smoker and let cool. The duck will continue to gain flavor the longer you let it rest — wrap it tightly in plastic wrap and refrigerate up to 1 week.

To make the mustard sauce, put the cream in a heavy saucepan, bring it to a boil and boil until reduced by half. Use a whisk to beat in the mustard, then remove the pan from the heat. Serve the sauce with the sliced smoked duck.

POULTRY & GAME DEALERS

Your best option for buying high-quality, organic poultry is to explore your area and establish a good relationship with your local butcher, retailer or farmer. Here is a list to get you started.

RETAILERS

WHOLE FOODS MARKET
Various locations in the U.S., Canada and the UK
www.wholefoodsmarket.com

ROWE FARMS
Toronto, ON, Canada
www.rowefarms.ca

THE HEALTHY BUTCHER
Ontario, Canada
www.thehealthybutcher.com

FARMS USA

BRICK HOUSE FARMS
Jim and Eve Lyle
1139 Brick House Road
Gaffney, SC 29340
tel: (864) 490.7108
www.brickhousefarms1943.com

COON CREEK FAMILY FARM
Vince & Julie Maro
Mondovi, WI
tel: (715) 834.4547
www.cooncreekfamilyfarm.com

COULEE VIEW FAMILY FARM
54247 Valentine Lane
Wauzeka, WI 53826
tel: (608) 874.4144
www.couleeviewfarm.com

CROSS TIMBERS RANCH
P.O. Box 1072
Franklin, TX 77856-1072
tel: (979) 777.1877
www.ctrtexas.com

DART CREEK FARM LTD.
61580 Gensman Road
Saint Helens, OR 97051
tel: (503) 397.9766
www.dartcreekfarm.com

DEE CREEK FARM
P.O. Box 1936
Woodland, WA 98674
tel: (360) 225.9711
www.deecreekfarm.com

GLACIAL ACRES
Jeremy & Kelly Lanctot
Sunburg MN 56289
tel: (320) 278.2002
www.glacialacres.com

HOFFMAN HATCHERY, INC.
P.O. Box 129
Gratz, PA 17030
www.hoffmanhatchery.com

J.M. HATCHERY
178 Lowry Road
New Holland, PA 17557
tel: (717) 354.5950
www.jmhatchery.com

L & A FAMILY FARMS
22331 Staley Rd.
Paris, IL 61944
tel: (217) 275.3380
www.lafamilyfarms.com

LEGACY MANOR FARM
17758 Bakersville Road
Boonsboro, MD 21713
tel: (301) 432.0267
www.legacymanorfarm.com

LITTLE PORTION MONASTERY FARM
350 County Road 248
Berryville, AR 72616
tel: (479) 253.7710 ext. 204
www.monasteryfarm.com

MACK HILL FARM
Frank and Lisa Richards
35 Mack Hill Road
P.O. Box 71
Marlow, NH 03456
tel: (603) 446.6261
www.mackhillfarm.com

MISTY MEADOWS FARM
215 Blevins Road
Payneville, KY 40157
tel: (270) 496.4218
www.packardsmmfarm.com

MOUNTAIN FORK FARM
1557 Mountain Fork Road
New Market, AL 35761
tel: (256) 379.4762
www.mountainforkfarm.com

NATURE'S HARBOR FARM
231 Fisher Rd
Foster, KY 41043
tel: (859) 472.1005
www.naturesharborfarm.com

S & G POULTRY, LLC
PO Box 2363
Clanton, AL 35046
tel: (205) 280.3771
www.sandgpoultry.com

SIMPLY ABUNDANT FARM
6890 Lost Country Lane
Richmond, VA 23231
tel: (804) 506.4015
www.simply-abundant.com

SO'JOURNEY FARM
1841 Bristoria Road
Holbrook, PA 15341
tel: (724) 499.5680
www.sojourneyfarm.com

STONE BARNS CENTER FOR
FOOD AND AGRICULTURE
630 Bedford Road
Pocantico Hills, NY 10591
tel: (914) 366.6200
www.stonebarnscenter.org

SUMAYAH'S PEACEFUL
POULTRY
1212 Haven Lane
Warfordsburg, PA 17267
tel: (631) 379.7314
www.peacefulpoultry.com

THISTLE BYRE FARM, INC.
P.O. Box 257
Delphi, IN 46923
tel: (765) 202.0100
www.thistlebyrefarm.com

TWENTY-FOUR RIVERS
Erik Schramm,
LLC Plant City, FL 33565,
www.twenty-fourrivers.com

WEED KNOB FARM
Peter & Stephanie Lizon
Laroy, WV 25252,
tel: (304) 273.2433
www.weedknob.com

WILDCRAFT FARMS, INC.
Ed & Christi Leonardi,
Swan Lake NY 12783
tel: (845) 292.0881
www.wildcraftfarms.com

WINDY RIDGE FARM
Tim & Kathy Koegel,
POB 1162 Alfred, NY 14802
tel: (607) 587.9684
www.windyridgepoultry.com

FARMS CANADA

BERETTA ORGANIC FARMS
80 Galaxy Blvd
Etobicoke, ON, Canada
M9W 4Y8
tel: (416) 674.5609
www.berettaorganics.com

FENWOOD FARM
John and Carol Fennema
774 Sawmill Road
R.R. #2,
Ancaster, ON, Canada
L9G 3L1
tel: (905) 765.1479
toll free: 1.800.373.7686
www.fenwoodfarm.com

KAWARTHA ECOLOGICAL
GROWERS
472 Farms Rd., R.R.#2
Woodville, ON, Canada
K0M 2T0
tel: (705) 439.3372
www.kawarthaecological
growers.com

LOVE THOSE WEEDS
17237 Quail Road
Monkland, ON, Canada
tel: (613) 360.6363
www.lovethoseweeds.ca

SMOKIN' IRON FARMS
11401 – 50th Street
Edmonton, AB, Canada
T5W 3B5
tel: (780) 471.0851
www.smokinironfarms.com

STODDART FAMILY FARM
1315 Zion Rd,
R.R. No. 2
Little Britain, ON, Canada
K0M 2C0
tel: (705) 786.7705
www.stoddart.ca

WHISPERING PINES FARM &
GARDEN
2941 Flos Rd 6W
Phelpston, ON, Canada
tel: (705) 322.6218

INDEX

DEDICATION
To the wonderful memories of my Nanna Foley

It's one of those things with acknowledgments that, should you mention someone and it is not enough, it is not enough, and should you not mention someone then you're doomed. This project started life as a book about game birds and waterfowl and is now one that specializes in the humble chicken. This I sometimes battle with, but I hope that you get great enjoyment from all the work that has gone into it by so many very talented people. Firstly, to the ever-patient and very wonderful Aussie who even under the effects of jet lag can function and is the best editor in all the world: Miss Jenni Muir — you rock and are bloody cool.

To all at Quadrille for taking the risk with me and this great book — especially to Claire Peters for standing, watching and turning this into a thing of beauty, and to Anne Furniss, many thanks. A really big thank you to all the people at Smiths and THE LUXE who cook, trial, test and toil — and just for being fab. To Tony Moyse — so cool and a great cook — and to Jason Lowe for his lovely work. Also a big thank you for those who I've forgotten or maybe just missed out on purpose!

A FIREFLY BOOK

Published by Firefly Books Ltd. 2010

Copyright © 2010 Quadrille Publishing Limited

First printing

Publisher Cataloging-in-Publication Data (U.S.)
Torode, John.
    Chicken / John Torode.
[256] p. : col. photos. ; cm.
Includes index.
Summary: Covering all aspects of buying and cooking chicken and other edible birds, with advice and recipes for chicken, turkey and game such as pigeon, pheasant and partridge.
ISBN-13: 978-1-55407-612-3 (pbk.)
ISBN-10: 1-55407-612-9 (pbk.)
1. Cookery (Poultry). 2. Cookery (Chicken). I. Title.
641.665 dc22   TX750.T676 2010

Library and Archives Canada Cataloguing in Publication
Torode, John
        Chicken / John Torode.
Includes index.
ISBN-13: 978-1-55407-612-3
ISBN-10: 1-55407-612-9
        1. Cookery (Poultry). I. Title.
TX750.T67 2009   641.6'65   C2009-905258-X

Published in the United States by
Firefly Books (U.S.) Inc.
P.O. Box 1338, Ellicott Station
Buffalo, New York 14205

Published in Canada by
Firefly Books Ltd.
66 Leek Crescent
Richmond Hill, Ontario L4B 1H1

Printed in China